D0375665

THE IDEA WRITERS

THE IDEA WRITERS

COPYWRITING
IN A NEW MEDIA
AND MARKETING ERA

Teressa Iezzi

palgrave
macmillan

THE IDEA WRITERS

Copyright © Crain Communications, Inc. 2010
All rights reserved.

First published in 2010 by PALGRAVE MACMILLAN® in the U.S.—a
division of St. Martin's Press LLC, 175 Fifth Avenue, New York, NY 10010.

Where this book is distributed in the UK, Europe and the rest of the world,
this is by Palgrave Macmillan, a division of Macmillan Publishers Limited,
registered in England, company number 785998, of Houndmills,
Basingstoke, Hampshire RG21 6XS.

Palgrave Macmillan is the global academic imprint of the above companies
and has companies and representatives throughout the world.

Palgrave® and Macmillan® are registered trademarks in the United States,
the United Kingdom, Europe and other countries.

ISBN: 978-0-230-61388-1

Library of Congress Cataloging-in-Publication Data
Iezzi, Teressa.
   The idea writers : copywriting in a new media and marketing era / by
Teressa Iezzi.
      p.   cm.
      ISBN 978-0-230-61388-1
   1. Advertising copy.   2. Marketing.   I. Title.
HF5825.I49   2011
659.14'4—dc22

                                                        2010035428

A catalogue record of the book is available from the British Library.

Design by Letra Libre

First edition: December 2010

10 9 8 7 6 5 4 3

Printed in the United States of America.

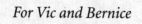

For Vic and Bernice

CONTENTS

ACKNOWLEDGMENTS

Clearly, *The Idea Writers* wouldn't have been possible without the idea writers—the copywriters, art directors, creative directors, producers and strategists who shared their insights, experiences and stories. I was humbled by their generosity and their smarts and can't thank them enough.

The agency PR people who helped organize so many interviews also deserve heaps of gratitude. They're busy people themselves and they helped wrangle some other extremely busy people, often managing to schedule interviews within laughable time frames.

I want to thank my comrade in *Creativity,* Ann Christine Diaz, for her ideas and for keeping the *Creativity* machine rolling while I worked on this project, and Laurie Harting from Palgrave Macmillan for her patience and guidance.

And, finally, Jonah Bloom, my mate (in both the British and the normal senses), editor and sounding board, without whose encouragement I wouldn't have finished or even started this project and without whose help and support I'd be curled up in a corner at this very moment, rocking and clutching at myself.

CHAPTER 1

THE CREATIVITY AGE

In 2006, *Esquire* magazine named ad man David Droga to its annual "Best and Brightest" list. As its name implies,[1] the list comprised walking superlatives only. The other 41 bright lights included Sebastian Thrun, an artificial intelligence expert pioneering self-driving cars; evolutionary biologist Paul Hebert; Hugh Herr, a prosthetics developer at MIT; and Princeton professor and creator of quantum-cascade lasers, Claire Gmachl.

Droga, then 37, had made a name for himself in the ad world for being ambitious and talented, and, perhaps as a result, fairly consistently successful. Having come from Nowhere, Australia (he once told *Creativity* magazine he grew up playing with wombats), Droga joined the ad industry as a copywriter in 1988 and became a creative director three years later, at age 21. From Australia he moved to Asia, heading up Saatchi & Saatchi's Singapore office and then in 1999, not yet 30, jumped to what was then the very epicenter of advertising creativity, Saatchi & Saatchi London. As the creative heart of the ad industry migrated from London to New York, so did he. He moved to the States in 2003 taking the global chief creative officer job at Publicis in New York and then, in 2004 made that ultimate leap, starting his own agency, Droga5 (the shop's name is a nod to his rank among six siblings; his mother sewed labels into the young Drogas' clothing, from Droga 1 to 6).

His admission into the aforementioned *Esquire* Best and Brightest club is evidence of how Droga's new company fared in its early days.

COPYWRITER'S TIP

SELF PROMOTION IS YOUR OTHER JOB

No one would accuse Droga, or many of the other high-profile creatives named in this book, of being publicity shy. This isn't a character flaw. This is advertising.

If you're a substance-over-style type, or Canadian, or not a Gen Y over-sharer, drawing attention to yourself might go against your grain. But it bears mentioning—if you have something to show for yourself, show it. Your job is making brands famous, and it behooves you to use some of your powers on yourself.

Having your own blog or other web presence goes without saying, as does participating in social media beyond the personal. Weigh in on Twitter on creative topics you care about. There are many, many blowhards in the ad business who have cultivated valuable personal brands based more on self promotion than any discernable talent or insight. You don't want to be them, but you can certainly learn from them.

This, it must be said, goes doubly for women, who have historically done a better job at the actual work they do than at trumpeting said work or themselves in general.

Seek out the reporters/bloggers/pundits covering the industry or sector you're interested in. If there are events where what you do will be discussed, put yourself forward as a speaker or panel member. If there's a story written about the kind of work you do, contact the writer and send her some of your work to keep in mind for next time.

Apply the same self promotion guidelines to your personal projects.

This applies before and after you get a job.

When Droga was selected for *Esquire*'s list, the magazine's editors, in addition to crafting the standard blurb detailing the nature and degree of his brightness, asked the honoree to put his pen where his reputation was. Droga was asked to demonstrate his advertising prowess by creating an ad to run in the issue, giving readers the opportunity, of course, to read his glowing profile, look at a manifestation of this alleged talent and think, "Meh." Faced with that sort of pressure, one can imagine Droga pausing for a deep breath and a moment of gratitude for his well-developed self-confidence.

Unsurprisingly, Droga filled the brief like a champ. His creation for that issue of *Esquire* went on to earn an armful of ad awards, including the coveted Titanium Lion from the International Advertising Festival, aka the Cannes Lions. It was talked about in mainstream media outlets from the *New York Times* and CNN to E! News. Even for Droga, getting that sort of result from a print ad with a headline, a simple graphic and some body copy seemed over the top.

Only it wasn't a print ad that attracted all that attention and acclaim. The thing that Droga created wasn't even an ad, exactly. It was a brand and a cause. It was an idea.

It was called Tap Project. Droga5 designer Ji Lee created a simple logo—a graphic representation of a blue tumbler of water looped by concentric circles, like ripples radiating beyond the glass. The logo represented a humanitarian campaign on behalf of UNICEF to help make clean drinking water accessible to the 1.1 billion people in the developing world without it. According to Droga's big idea, to help those people, New Yorkers had only to do what they frequently did anyway—go to a restaurant and order a glass of tap water with their meal. Those who dined out in New York on World Water Day, March 22, could ask for water in vessels labeled with the Tap Project logo, and add $1 to their bill for the privilege, with the proceeds going to UNICEF's clean water efforts. Droga's agency recruited all of the city's top chefs and restaurateurs and local celebrities, including Sarah Jessica Parker, who became the spokesperson for UNICEF's clean water cause.

By March 22, over 300 New York restaurants were in on the effort. There was a site, tapproject.com, where people could learn about the campaign and see a list of restaurants and endorsements by chefs and celebrities, there was a fundraising event, there was a print initiative that saw magazines from *Esquire* to *New York* running essays on water from well-known authors, there were commercials and web films, retail tie-ins—designer Donna Karan created Tap shirts and drinking glasses—and there were millions and millions of dollars of PR as broadcast, print and online media outlets in New York and around the world spread the word about this simple, inarguable idea.

In 2008, after the inaugural campaign in New York, seven U.S. ad agencies were recruited to create their own campaigns, which they did in 30 North American cities. By 2009, 100 cities around the world were involved in the project. The initial Tap campaign reached over 80 million people (based on Nielsen ratings) and, according to UNICEF, generated $5.5 million for its cause. All with $0 spent on media.

So, what was wrong with just creating a nice print ad and leaving it at that?

"I'm in the business of building brands, so as an exercise, I wanted to see if I could build a brand from a single-page ad out of nothing and create something," Droga told *Creativity* at the time.

With Tap, Droga created something that engaged people on their own terms, encouraged participation and sharing and involved a range of platforms; something that, rather than having a start and an end date, like an ad campaign, was a living, breathing, open-ended enterprise. That he did so speaks of the monumental changes in the ad industry and the potentially limitless scope of the copywriter's job. It should be noted that Droga was by no means unique in looking beyond the printed page—it's no coincidence that at the time the Tap Project was created, magazine ad revenues (including *Esquire's*) were in precipitous decline, and the entire print industry was, and remains, in crisis mode. Clearly, other entities have come to the conclusion that a two-dimensional print ad, while still a valid means of communication, is not the last word in connecting a brand with consumers.

In the end, yes, there was a print ad in that issue of *Esquire*. Droga and agency executive creative director Ted Royer, both copywriters by trade, and designer Lee, assisted by junior creatives Amanda Clellend and Jesse Juriga, created that ad and the copy and the FAQs on the web site and the scripts in the TV spots that would be created after the fact to boost awareness of the campaign.

But, first, a copywriter created a brand, a new means of fund raising and a new platform for UNICEF. A copywriter, working with a group of creatives and producers, rallied the New York culinary community, and created a cultural phenomenon.

All these things, and more, now fall under the general job description of the copywriter. In other words, a copywriter does a lot more today than write copy. And copy can be a lot more than a headline or TV script.

"Writers now are less typecast than before," says Droga. "They are not restricted to headlines, dialogue and body copy. An idea may be born from an inspiring manifesto or business idea. Something that informs everything a brand does from that day forward."

The copywriter's job has changed as much as the advertising industry itself. And, no matter what the old bastards[2] say, that change has been fundamental, irrevocable and, to many players in the media and marketing scene, catastrophic. "We are an industry built on assumptions that no longer exist today," says Droga.

Those assumptions include the following: that pushing out a Big Marketing Campaign that runs for several weeks and then stops is the best way to connect a brand to consumers; that a large media budget assures a marketer of getting its message across to its desired audience; that one-way, TV-borne messages are the only, or even the primary, or even a necessary unit of marketing; that big ad agencies with global tentacles and lots of awards in their reception areas will always own the primary relationship with a marketer; that people only watch media-company-made content at media-company-dictated times; that professional ad people are the only people who can tell brand stories; and that anyone gives a good goddamn about what you're telling them in your ads.

All of the entities—including large ad agencies, magazines and newspapers, TV networks and media conglomerates, creatives, CEOs and advertisers—that had worked successfully under the assumptions that governed the previous era are no longer guaranteed success, or even survival, in this new era. And while calling this era the Digital Era adequately describes the basic media shift that's taken place, calling it the Consumer Control Era probably gets closer to the rub, better describing the essential, overwhelming change that is remaking the industry and the copywriting profession.

THE TV ADVERTISING AGE

There are many books and other resources that you can and should read that provide detailed analyses of the transformation of media, culture and marketing and the great trials that have been visited on advertising.[3]

For now, here is a somewhat reductive rundown.

The advertising industry, since its beginning in the mid 1800s,[4] revolved around creating brand messages that were adjacent to or small interruptions in the content that people were watching, reading, listening to, looking at—the (easily avoided) price of admission to the main attraction. Ad agency writers and art directors created these short messages, and the ad agency that employed them (and later, the agency's giant media buying operation, spun out to make maximum profit for the shareholders who owned the holding company that owned the agency) bought media space to place the ad in proximity to content that would be seen, presumably, by an audience of pre-determined size and composition. For the first part of advertising history, this exercise revolved mainly around print, and most of the classic copywriting books deal with creating ads for this medium. For the next part, and until recently, for most creatives advertising has equaled TV commercials.

From the late 1950s to roughly 2002, TV was the media sun. It was the focal point for marketers, agencies, creatives and the public. TV came to so dominate the media landscape in North America that most big agencies remade themselves, their processes, their structure and their talent base around making TV commercials.

During the TV years, the best copywriters made 30-second spots into art, or something that looked an awful lot like it. They crafted narratives that used combinations of humor, beautiful imagery, music and emotion to convey a human truth and join the soul of a brand with the heart of the consumer. Every so often, a talented writer would create a new style of advertising that fed from and in turn influenced the larger entertainment and cultural world. They created tag lines that became part of popular culture ("Where's the Beef?" "Just Do It." "Got Milk?" "There's An App For That." "I'm On A Horse." All created by once and future copywriting legends). Their work informed our childhoods and formed part of our collective consciousness.

But, lest we risk over-romanticizing, we should remember that those memorable hall-of-fame ads were and are the exception. The ratio of good to bad ads, good to bad anything, is probably immutable. Watch TV for a few hours. How many ads are good? Somewhere between 10 and 20 percent? That's the same as it ever was. And those people who tell you it was better back in the day? Don't believe them. For every "Think Small" in the '60s there was a bottomless bowl of the same insufferable dross that's served up on any given commercial break and that covers the ground from forgettable waste of everyone's time and money to actively annoying disincentive to ever buy the product being advertised. But who cared? TV was a blunt instrument. If you bought enough weight and aired your ad with the right frequency, you stood a decent chance of selling some stuff—though you stood an excellent chance of spending a big chunk of change.

But that was then—when the medium guaranteed a mass audience.

The media landscape during the TV years was a nice, finite, understandable, ownable place. In 1980, the "big three" networks, ABC, CBS and NBC, garnered more than 90 percent of prime-time TV-viewing eyeballs. By 2005, this share was 32 percent. And that just reflects the shift in audience among those who were still watching TV; in other words, it basically covers the explosion of TV outlets and cable. Since the go-go '80s, the media universe has exploded into an almost infinite number of small pieces, on and off TV. And by the time broadcast TV was succumbing to cable, the internet was, effectively, becoming the center of people's media world.

You know some version of the basic stats by now—YouTube, launched in December 2005, now serves two billion videos daily; Facebook gained 500 million users in its first six years of life; Twitter has exploded, going from inexplicable habit of the young, self-absorbed media early adopter to acutely mainstream (see @aplusk, @kimkardashian) habit of everybody, and a key part of the social presence of brands. The rise of so-called social media made the sharing of opinions, of creativity, of everything, easy and accessible to every demographic.

"We are living in the middle of the largest increase in expressive capability in the history of the human race," said New York University Interactive Telecommunications Program professor Clay Shirky in his 2008 book on social media and technology-enabled cooperation, *Here Comes Everybody.* "More people can communicate more things to more people than has ever been possible in the past, and the size and speed of this increase, from under one million participants to over one billion in a generation, makes the change unprecedented, even considered against the background of previous revolutions in communications tools."

At a gathering of the Association of National Advertisers in 2009, Google CEO Eric Schmidt put it this way: "We now generate as much information every two days as was generated from the beginning of time to 2003."

As media options became limitless, it grew harder to reach huge numbers of people, or even smaller numbers of people in the same places in the same way. Even a marketer with a vast media budget could not guarantee mass audience reach by buying 30- or 60-second commercial slots. The current reality is that while TV is still a powerful tool of reach and a valuable component of a media plan, it is no longer—with the exception of the Super Bowl, which was watched in 2009 by about 98 million people—a truly mass reach vehicle. And TV commercials are certainly one thing, but not the only thing, that copywriters are or should be creating.

As the ad industry's model started to warp before its eyes, its answer was swift and sure. And that answer was: creativity! We have to make better, more creative commercials to cut through the clutter. Well, yes. That is correct, sort of, but it tragically misses the point at the same time. Creativity is certainly the right answer. But to say that the industry's job, the copywriter's job, now is to make better commercials is like saying a rodeo clown's job is to wear a red nose and a painted frown.

An important assumption, to be sure—but there is lots more to be done.

And this is where things get interesting for the new copywriter. The Consumer Control Era has meant that creatives must make things that people want, that they seek out and share with their circle, or with the world. It has meant that the marketing end game has transcended reach, just grabbing eyeballs, and it has become a matter of engagement, of inviting a conversation and making a meaningful, ongoing connection. And, while yes, any copywriter worthy of the title strives to make better ads, now those "ads" can be almost anything—a film, a TV show, a mobile app, a blog, a retail experience, a product, a song, a game, a distribution idea, a tweet, a scheme to get people to pay for tap water.

BEYOND THE ADVERTISING AGE

The growth and influence of the internet didn't simply add a new vehicle for clutter and make it harder to grab a consumer's attention. It completely and irreversibly transformed the media landscape and the way people experienced and interacted with brands and brand communications.

In the simplest terms, consumers gained an unprecedented degree of control over their media environment and the terms by which they would interact with any content, ad messages included.

With the advent of DVRs, of course, consumers could bypass brand messages on TV—a medium that was now fragmented into tiny shards of content. But ad avoidance is just the beginning. More to the point, consumers could and did get their information about brands, and everything else, from other consumers, from a massive range of sources online. And they could share their own information and reviews, too.

If they wanted to, and they often did, consumers could be producers of brand information, opinion, and, yes, advertising.

In 2007, Nick Haley, an 18-year-old student from the U.K. created his own interpretation of an Apple ad for the iTouch—simply a series of stock Apple images cut to the track "Music Is My Hot Hot Sex" by CSS. He posted the video to YouTube, where it was viewed by thousands of people, including people from Apple, who had their ad agency TBWA\Chiat\Day L.A. contact Haley and bring him to its Los Angeles HQ to help make a broadcast version of the spot. That same year, Doritos enlisted civilians to create its most high-profile ads of the year in its "Crash the Super Bowl" campaign. There are countless other examples of brands soliciting ideas from consumers. "Consumer-generated content" became one of the biggest (and, typically for the ad industry, misunderstood and poorly utilized) phenomena of the mid-00s.

But consumers weren't just generating videos. Several marketers harnessed consumer opinion to inform all areas of their product and service development, as well as marketing. Dell, for example, created IdeaStorm in 2007, a site where the public can contribute ideas on all aspects of Dell's offering, with a Digg-like system of promoting ideas to determine their popularity. Crowdsourcing, a term used first in a 2006 *Wired* article,[5] became the next ad industry darling and is, of course, used and abused with the usual abandon.

In November 2009, marketing behemoth Unilever yanked its Peperami (which is, essentially, a Euro beef jerky) account from longtime agency Lowe and announced it would "crowdsource" creative—posting the ad brief on a site called IdeaBounty.com and offering $10,000 to whomever submitted the winning idea. Unilever acknowledged that it wasn't looking for random rank amateurs to take on the brief; it was counting on bona fide ad creatives to contribute their more informed ideas. Shortly thereafter, two senior execs from top creative agency Crispin Porter + Bogusky announced they were exiting to start a new shop, Victors & Spoils, built around a crowdsourcing model.

And what a creative person with a broadband connection can giveth, a creative person with a broadband connection and a beef can also taketh away. Ad legend Bill Bernbach said that a great ad campaign would make a bad product fail faster. But even bad products could have a longer shelf life in the days before Twitter and YouTube.

Did you have a disappointing experience with a product or some aspect of a marketer's service? In the TV era, maybe you introduced a few new colorful words and phrases to a customer service rep over the phone. Maybe you wrote a letter. Maybe you gnashed your teeth and shook with impotent rage. In the Consumer Control Era, your rage can be told. In seconds, you can tell your 500 closest friends, who can then, by way of their social grid, or YouTube or countless other means, tell millions.

"United Breaks Guitars" is an especially inspiring example of the power of creativity and social media when wielded by an unhappy customer. United Airlines passenger and musician Dave Carroll complained that his Taylor guitar was willfully destroyed by the airline's baggage handlers during a flight in 2008. After United repeatedly declined to compensate him for the damage, he wrote a wonderfully catchy song decrying the airline's customer service and made an entertaining music video featuring his band, his guitar and some actors playing some comically callous United staff and posted it to YouTube. Ten days after it launched, the video was viewed by 3.2 million people and elicited 14,000 comments. It has since been viewed nearly 9 million times. In the aftermath of this video's explosion on the web, United's stock price sank more than 10 percent. Did one man's opinion, expressed engagingly and distributed for free to millions of people wipe $180 million off the airline's market cap? We may never know. But we do know that 9 million people have a worse impression of United than they did before (if such a thing is possible). And all the lovely, lyrical advertising in the world isn't going to change that.

And so with more consumer control, more mechanisms for interaction and sharing of opinion and content, the best marketers today focus on making the entire brand experience better—from product to packaging, service and ads. They do so not only to avoid the wrath of the disgruntled, but in the realization that there is no more powerful marketing tool than a happy customer.

One need only look at marketers like Amazon and Google and Zappos to get an empirical sense of the new scope and realities of marketing and brand creativity. None of those companies is known for advertising, but all have built fearsomely powerful brands. All have built their success based on a great product and customer experience, and evolving their service to respond to and often anticipate changes in the marketplace and in consumer behavior. When Amazon saw the Digital Era doing to book publishing what it's done to music and journalism, it didn't create an ad campaign to persuade people to keep buying printed books. It created the Kindle.

So what's a copywriter to do? Do consumer-generated content and crowdsourcing mean no more "professional" creatives? Does the decline of TV commercials mean the decline of copywriting? Does the explosion of consumer data mean marketing is all science and no creativity? Does the changing power dynamic among agencies and other creative companies mean no more places to work? Unsurprisingly, this book will suggest that all of those questions can be answered with a firm "no." You heard Eric Schmidt. There's a lot of content being made, and brands are going to be responsible for making a bigger and bigger share of it.

For copywriters, as much as for any other actor in the theater of marketing, this era represents a completely new range of challenges—copywriters are, after all, doing the doing, literally inventing the ideas that will shape not just their clients' marketing presence but the next phase of the evolution of the industry. And the general rulebook that's governed advertising affairs for over a hundred years has been thrown out. But, for that reason, it's also a more exciting and potentially creatively rewarding time than copywriters have seen since Bill Bernbach put art directors and copywriters together and proved that effective advertising could be witty, quotable and uplifting rather than a dreary recitation of "unique selling points." In fact, many people call this era the next creative revolution. Copywriters occupy vast creative territory—from the biggest business-building idea to the word on the screen. They now have the opportunity not only to reach people via an almost limitless array of channels, but they have the chance, the responsibility even, to make things that people like, and that maybe even make people's lives better.

"The role of the writer (the term copywriter probably ought to be retired) hasn't changed so much as it has expanded," says Joyce King Thomas, former EVP/CCO of McCann Erickson New York and the author of the famed "Priceless" campaign for MasterCard. As Mark Waites, the founder and CCO of top British agency Mother says, "it used to be that as a copywriter you mainly did TV spots and print ads and your job was to just get better and better at doing that. Now you have to keep learning entirely new things all the time."

If you work at an ad agency, those things might mean making an outrageously entertaining and successful ad that is viewed 10 million times on YouTube and puts a new brand on the map. Or it might mean doing a lot of work that couldn't be considered advertising in any historical sense.

Some of the best agencies now struggle with the very label of "advertising," with the idea that they are in the business of doing what we've always called advertising.

Lee Clow, the chairman and global director of TBWA Worldwide and creative godfather of TBWA\Chiat\Day is fond of saying that "everything is media," and has worked to retool his ad agency as a Media Arts Lab.

Many agencies now are as likely to be turning out an app or a web experiment as a commercial, and some are expanding further still, developing their own products and services.

"We're not in the advertising business," says Rob Reilly, co-chief creative officer at Crispin Porter + Bogusky, an agency that has dedicated significant resources to building its digital capability, and more recently, has developed a product innovation arm. "We're not an advertising agency anymore. We're in the business of invention. Copywriters are inventors."

Whatever labels they use, the best agencies realize that the value of their offering isn't tied to one medium any more than Amazon is in the business of paper. Their function is building brands. Always has been. In fact, many would argue that today's new model ad agency is more similar in terms of the scope of its work to the agencies of yore, which handled everything from package design to point of sale before the TV juggernaut made it profitable to create silos and to place certain tasks "above the line" and certain tasks "below the line."

Alex Bogusky, the creative force behind Crispin Porter + Bogusky (who recently exited the industry) told *Creativity* that the agency "is often seen as doing new things" with its early adoption of digital and its forays into product design. "But when I look at the history of advertising we're really just trying to grab back the old things that agencies gave up over the years. . . . I don't think we're all that newfangled. Everyone will have to have serious digital capabilities. To me [design] is very much the same thing. We're beginning a process of something that clients will expect."

One of CP+B's most significant product design efforts involved creating a fast food menu item for one of its marquee clients, Burger King. Chicken Fries (pretty much what you think they are—like french fries only chicken) began as a "hare-brained idea" from Reilly, a copywriter. Since their launch in 2004, they've become one of BK's most successful newer products. Says Bogusky, "You could probably argue that Chicken Fries has done more for BK's business than any amount of advertising we've done."

Wait, what?

Yes, you may want to go back and read that last bit again, but only after you've considered the following: that the quote comes from one of the most successful advertising players on the planet; that CP+B has done advertising for BK for seven years; that the agency has produced some of the industry's most popular, award-winning and effective work for this brand; that the shop's "Have it Your Way"–themed campaigns perfectly captured the spirit of the Consumer Control Age and that several of them became pop-culture sensations. Bogusky's quote is one giant mouthful as a summary of the reality of advertising, of the challenges ahead for agencies—and creatives—working within a so-called advertising agency.

And ad agencies, as mentioned, aren't the only creative partner for brands and not the only entities availing themselves of the services of copywriters. Look around: while a glance at today's media menu might indicate we're not necessarily becoming more literate as a culture (*Paul Blart: Mall Cop* was the top grossing film in America for the three weeks after it was released in the summer of 2009), there's more just plain writing everywhere. Technorati tracked 112

million blogs in 2008, (which doesn't include over 70 million Chinese blogs). There are millions of brand sites and microsites, incal-
culable amounts of video, over 50,000 apps (in the iPhone store only),
and 105 million Twitter accounts sending 50 million tweets per day
(as of April 2010); there are just more things to write.

And there are more places for writers to work and more opportunities for writers to work for themselves

Full-service ad agencies as we know them ruled the twentieth
century largely untouched. There are a broader range of creative
companies working in today's marketing arena, and as marketers
look for more holistic solutions, many of those companies are expanding the scope of the creative services they offer. So-called digital agencies, which rose with the internet, were originally website-
and banner-building specialists, an afterthought in the big brand
picture. If advertising was sexy and exciting, digital was . . . well, it
had a good personality. Now, many of these digital players are as di-
versified in discipline as many ad agencies, and as sexy—many are
the primary creative partner to marketers. Production companies,
once just hired to execute TV ads, more and more have a hand in
conceiving ideas as well. Design companies are, in many cases, taking on a bigger marketing role. And a whole new range of creative
startups have launched to challenge the bigger legacy agencies. Like
Droga5, they profess media agnosticism, idea-first thinking, an entrepreneurial philosophy and a disregard for TV-era boundaries re-
garding roles and job descriptions.

If you look at the output of all of these entities over the past few
years, you'll see more and more meaningful manifestations of change.
For the first part of the 00s, it seemed there was more talk about what
was happening or about to happen than there was appreciable action.
The past few years, though, have seen an explosion in the volume and
variety of multi-platform, or integrated, or whatever you want to call
it ideas from the formerly-known-as ad industry.

Perhaps the most accessible lens through which to view the shift
in industry end product is that of award-show results. Like most industries, adland is in love with loving itself. We will save a discussion
of whether this preoccupation with self-congratulation is harmful or
helpful and the real versus the perceived value of awards for later, but
for now, consider awards useful as a barometer of creative evolution.

First, for most of advertising history, the climax of any award show was the Grand Prize for best TV spot. When agencies began producing online and other "non-traditional" work, the award shows added categories for digital, and when agencies' work started getting more integrated, more complicated, and extending through more platforms, they added more categories. The Cannes Advertising Festival, for example, added the somewhat comically named Cyber category in 1998, and in 2005 it tacked on the Titanium category to recognize a new kind of innovative and/or multi-platform work that didn't fit into any one media bucket. Shortly after it was launched, the Titanium Lion replaced the Film Grand Prix as the most coveted accolade in all of advertising. Winning best spot was great, but the cool kids (and the agencies that seemed to be winning a lot of new business) won Titaniums.

Here are some of the campaigns that have won Titanium Lions:

Burger King Games
The games are a series of three XBox console games based around the Burger King "King" character created by Crispin Porter + Bogusky. BK customers actually paid for the games—$3.99 each—and ended up buying 2 million units, sales figures that rivaled results for XBox titles like Call of Duty 3, released in the same holiday season.

Million
An even more ambitious effort from Droga5, Million is a campaign to improve the New York City public education system by using the very bane of every teacher's existence—the mobile phone. The initiative sought to give every public school kid a special phone that delivers lessons and extra help and rewards performance with free goodies, like food and music downloads. Crucially, one thing the phones do not do is allow calls or texts during class.

Nike+
A collaboration between Nike, Apple and Nike's digital agency R/GA, Nike+ was a product—a piece of kit you put in your shoe to track running data.

Fiat eco:Drive
Created for automaker Fiat by digital agency AKQA, eco:Drive is a system that uses a computer application and an in-car USB port to mine driving data and calculate driving efficiency to recommend ways a driver can reduce fuel costs and carbon emissions.

The 2008 Barack Obama presidential campaign

These initiatives represent an industry in transition. They represent the creative contributions of a range of different creative companies and individuals; they represent ideas that aren't just attractive to award-show judges (i.e., other ad creatives). They are ideas that mean something to consumers, to the viewing, playing, learning, driving and voting public.

And they are exciting for what they represent for writers.

There was, however, one creative milestone that predated all of these ad landmarks and that, in its own way, changed the brand debate more than the most innovative, most watched, most awarded piece of communications. And that was the iPod. What does the iPod have to do with copywriting? Indirectly, everything. Because the success of Apple's incendiary device demonstrated, at a time when the industry needed it spelled out, the power of the complete brand experience, where everything from the packaging to the shape and feel of the product, to the color of the headphones, to the spots worked together to create one cohesive identity. Sure the ads, by TBWA\Chiat\Day L.A. (and now Chiat\Day's Media Arts Lab), were superb. The first major campaign, depicting silhouetted dancers shaking it to edgy tracks wearing the trademark white ear buds, became a cultural phenomenon. But the ads were just one part of the overall creative experience that was iPod. And the creative experience started and ended and was fully, completely informed by design.

The iPod was also a gorgeous little symbol of the complete destruction and reinvention of a business sector—the music industry. And it would signal the start of a creative/destructive wave that would wash over TV, film, journalism and, of course, advertising.

And, not for nothing, but the iPod wouldn't be the iPod without the work of a writer. It was freelance copywriter Vinnie Chieco who is responsible for the product's epoch-defining name.

As we know, the iPod was only the start. There were more game-changing gadgets, more dangerous ideas that came after, and there are more that will be unleashed in the coming days and weeks.

Point being, the changes that are happening now are only a whisper of a suggestion of a taste of what's to come. And the job of the copywriter is going to keep changing apace. Does that mean there are no longer any constants, any bedrock principles to guide a copywriter through jobs and through a career? That's what we'll address in the following pages.

CHAPTER 2

BERNBACH TO THE FUTURE

"It is spring and I am blind."

If you want to begin a discussion of the fundamentals of copywriting, to distill the job down to some rich, primordial essence, a simple declaration by a sightless man on a sunny day is a good place to start. In the annals of advertising writing, the line is doctrine. It's part of the copywriting canon. It's an ad legend that's transcended advertising, evoked by everyone from salesmen to motivational speakers.

The line is attributed to David Ogilvy, the ad titan who gave the world the eye-patch-sporting man in the Hathaway shirt and advertising aphorisms like "the consumer is not a moron, she's your wife." As the story goes, on his way into work one morning (one imagines the dapper, imposing Brit striding up Madison like an Ayn Rand hero, a gray-flanneled monument to his own will), Ogilvy encountered a homeless man begging on the street with a sign that read "I am blind. Please help." Ogilvy paused before the unfortunate, noticing the empty cup at his side and, rather than making a monetary contribution, he took the man's sign and rewrote it (because, like any Randian hero, he eschewed charity and always carried a Sharpie).

When Ogilvy left his office later that day, the homeless man's cup, naturally, was overflowing.

The story, which most agree is apocryphal, is the ur-example of the Truth Well Told, and, in the simplest way, advertising as storytelling. After the ministrations of the ad man, the beggar's sign no longer just conveyed information and asked for action, like Buy Now, Get $2 Off. With a few, very few, well-chosen words in a specific context, the sign told a story. It played to imagination, memory and emotion.

Nobody can read the phrase "It is spring and I am blind" without conjuring their own springtime memories and associations and without a pang of sadness or empathy for a poor man, warmed by a pale sun and teased by the wafting perfume of flowers and pretty girls he cannot see.

David Ogilvy and some of the other greats we'll discuss in this chapter shaped advertising as we know it. Through the ads they wrote and the books about their work, they've been teachers to generations of writers. In light of the grand reordering discussed in chapter 1, are the lessons of the ad giants still relevant? Yes, indeed. But as much as some basic aspects of human nature and writing remain unchanged from the previous ad era, there have been some fundamental, unprecedented shifts that have changed the world and the work of the copywriter.

THE LORDS OF INFORMATION

Ogilvy is, of course, considered a giant among copywriters and in the history of advertising in general.

He reigned in the 1950s and occupied an interesting point of inflection in the history of the ad business. As one of the few advertising names that has some stature in the cultural world outside advertising, Ogilvy is considered a creative luminary but he only reluctantly called himself a "creative." In fact, he fairly scoffed at the whole notion of creativity in his second book, *Ogilvy on Advertising*. Under the heading "The Cult of Creativity" he wrote: "The Benton & Bowles agency holds that 'If it doesn't sell, it isn't creative.' Amen. . . . You won't find 'creativity' in the 12-volume Oxford Dictionary. Do you think it means originality? Says [Rosser] Reeves: 'Originality is the most dangerous word in advertising.' I occasionally use the hideous word creative, myself, for lack of a better. If you take the subject more seriously than I do, I suggest you read *The Creative Organization*. Meanwhile, I have to invent a Big Idea for a new advertising campaign, and I have to invent it before Tuesday. 'Creativity' strikes me as a high-falutin' word for the work I have to do between now and Tuesday."[1]

To put it simply, many of your Big Swinging Ad Legends up to this point had a very strictly research- and information-driven approach to making ads.

Ogilvy himself was a research man for Gallup for ten years (and, incidentally, didn't write his first ad until he was 39, so it's never too late!).

But if his most famous ads are the measure, Ogilvy knew the power of story. The Hathaway eye patch itself, he said, added "story appeal" to the print campaign's photographs of the manly yet aristocratic Baron George Wrangell wearing the hell out of those crisp collared shirts. It was Ogilvy who famously purchased the eye patch on the way to the first photo shoot and insisted, over client objections, on including it in the ad.

But Ogilvy was, in many ways, of the same school as Rosser Reeves, who is considered one of the fathers of modern advertising, a pioneer in writing for the emerging media of television and the man responsible for the idea of the Unique Selling Proposition (USP). Both men were devotees of Claude Hopkins, author of *Scientific Advertising*.

Like Hopkins, Reeves was a hard seller. He believed that every word uttered or written on behalf of a brand should serve in doing one thing—selling the product—and that an ad should get straight to the business of doing just that. He believed that advertising should identify a singular characteristic that distinguished a product from its competitors and convey that advantage to people as directly as possible, to the point of repetition. Recall was paramount, and he tested copy relentlessly to determine which words stuck in heads and which didn't. Reeves believed that ads should deliver one simple, clear idea— buy this product, get this specific benefit—and that visual or narrative bells and whistles were merely distractions (vampires, he called them) that would drain effectiveness. He also believed that ad campaigns shouldn't change over time. Reeves said in his book *Reality in Advertising* that "the art of advertising was getting a message into the heads of the most people at the lowest possible cost."

The use of the word "art" here is misleading though. Reeves had no time for art, or "fine writing."[2] In the classic copywriting book *The Art of Writing Advertising*, Reeves has a comically heated exchange with his interviewer on the subject of the "artsy-craftsy" inclinations of certain ad people and on awards and industry self-congratulation. His interlocutor, a former *Advertising Age* editor, suggests that ad awards, perhaps rightly, acknowledged that there can be a craft, a beauty, to copywriting beyond banging away at a USP. Reeves can barely contain himself. He asks the interviewer to assume the vantage point of a hypothetical marketer whose sales are falling and asks: "What do you want out of me? Do you want fine writing? Do you want masterpieces? Do you want glowing things that can be framed by copywriters? Or do you want to see the goddamn sales curve stop moving down and start moving up? What do you want?"

This is a man who would spontaneously combust were he to witness the orgy of creativity and self love that is the Cannes advertising festival and some of the, shall we say, artful brand image campaigns that claim its highest honors today.

Reeves, whose career is said to be the inspiration for the Don Draper character on *Mad Men*, held sway through the 1950s. Perhaps his best-known ad and USP is M&Ms' "Melts in Your Mouth Not in Your Hand"—to this day one of the most culturally embedded ad slogans. Even Reeves, who believed in the eternal qualities of a great campaign, could scarcely have envisioned the reach of his work (or that it would be appropriated by no less a cultural icon than Curtis "50 Cent" Jackson, who conveyed his own USP when he rapped in his 2005 hit "Candy Shop": "I'm trying to explain baby the best way I can / I melt in your mouth girl, not in your hands").

"WE'RE RIGHT ABOUT EVERYTHING BUT NOBODY LOOKS"

But by the mid 1960s Reeves was retired. And so, it seemed, was his philosophy of advertising.

At the end of the '50s, Bill Bernbach and his crew at Doyle Dane Bernbach in New York were making much of the advertising of the day seem repetitive, annoying, bordering on insulting. Which, of course, it was. Just like most ads today.

Bernbach had, earlier in his career, worked with design legend Paul Rand; the pair were said to be the first copywriter/art director team. And that set the tone for his professional life. Bernbach and his famous creatives, including art directors Bob Gage, George Lois and Helmut Krone, and copywriters Phyllis Robinson, Julian Koenig and, later, Mary Wells Lawrence, created advertising that was strikingly different for its time, much of it famous to this day and revered by generations of copywriters. The groundbreaking Volkswagen "Think Small" print ad; Avis "We Try Harder"; "You Don't Have to be Jewish to Like Levy's" for Levy's Bakery; "He likes it! Hey Mikey" for Life Cereal. The hits kept on coming.

For many copywriters and other ad practitioners who came of age after him, Bill Bernbach is the north, the south, the east, the west, the immortal, the all. And for good reason. Bernbach represented creativity, originality, the art of advertising. Reeves represented information, repetition, testing. If Reeves was "Head On: Apply Directly to the Forehead!," Bernbach was Guinness "Surfer." (The thing to keep in mind for later: both of those ads worked.)

COPYWRITER'S TIP

DO WHAT NO ONE ELSE WANTS TO DO

Tom Carty and his partner Walter Campbell, who created Guinness "Surfer," weren't even supposed to be working on the Guinness account at the time. As a creative team at Abbott Mead Vickers BBDO in London, they were hungry, and they offered to work when no one else wanted to—over the holidays. That's when they came up with the famous line Good Things Come to Those Who Wait. This isn't an argument for abandoning your family at the holidays (though that may be a pleasant result for you). But it's a plug for being proactive, for wading into the weeds, for, well, working pretty hard.

Bernbach believed that advertising had to offer an entertaining reason for people to even acknowledge its existence. Referring to a study at the time that said that 85 percent of ads went unnoticed, he said "I think the most important thing in advertising is to be original and fresh . . . Because you can have all the right things in an ad, and if nobody is made to stop and listen to you, you've wasted it. And we in America are spending so darn much money for efficiency, to measure things, that we're achieving boredom like we've never achieved before. We're right about everything, but nobody looks."[3]

So, for many creatives today, Bernbach's lessons are the most relevant for today's over-saturated media world.

But—and this will scandalize faithful students of either ad school—the differences between the Reeves and Bernbach approaches aren't that significant in relative terms. That is, they aren't that significant compared to the broader difference between advertising as all of the men and women of that era knew it, and advertising as you, the modern copywriter, are practicing it today. When DDB started creating ads like "Lemon," it was called the creative revolution. But that description is an overstatement. The real revolution is happening now.

THE CONSUMER CONTROL ERA

We know that today's copywriter works in ideas, creating content and experiences that play out across multiple platforms, and working in media that Reeves and those who came after him couldn't have imagined.

But that's missing the larger point about the real creative revolution. There has been a more elemental shift from then to now that should inform the work of the copywriter.

While Reeves or Ogilvy would have claimed to be at odds with Bernbach about the issue of "creativity," the truth was that they were all great copywriters who lived at a time when they could push one powerful message to a large audience. In the '50s and '60s and up until the late '90s, whatever your philosophy, advertising meant a specific thing: creating a one-way piece of communications about a brand and putting it on a particular media channel, typically adjacent to a piece of "real" content. As Howard Gossage, another revered copywriting figure from the late '50s and '60s, said, "when advertising talks about its audience, it doesn't mean its audience, it means somebody else's, gathered there to watch or read something else."[4]

Whether the ad conveyed some unique piece of information about what a product could do for you, or grabbed your attention with sex, or made you smile makes little difference. There was a basic exchange—brand A paid an ad agency and a media outlet in order to tell a number of people what they should think about their brand, or some aspect of it. The people were probably exposed to brand A's message. They listened or didn't listen. They bought the product or didn't buy the product. The end.

Today, brands and agencies aren't in control of that fundamental exchange in the same way anymore. Consumers are in control of what media they consume and when and, more and more, they are in control of what other consumers think about brands. Brand messaging is no longer one-way, and there are many, many more options for consumers than simply listen, don't listen, buy or don't buy. Here are just a few of them: watch; listen; play; create a parody that is viewed by more people than the original ad; create a Facebook page that exposes one of your business practices and that urges people not to buy your product; create a site devoted to praising your customer service; add a review of your product to a popular site; post a video of your customer service representative sleeping in their living room instead of fixing your cable; create a site devoted to alternatives for your product that are better for the environment; create your entire ad campaign.

In the era of consumer control, consumers aren't just consumers. They're producers, they're critics, they're creatives. In Clay Shirky's 2010 book, *Cognitive Surplus*, they are referred to as "the people formerly known as the audience." This is the essential shift that resulted from the digital revolution, and the essential truth that should inform the work of today's copywriter.

In advertising's past, advertisers could, at least to some extent, control their image in the eyes of consumers. Today, advertisers live in a transparent world. The dissonance between a company or brand's ad-burnished image and the reality of how its product really works and how it does business is clear for everyone to see.

The entire brand experience—from product to packaging and retail presence, from customer service to communications—is subject to scrutiny and is part of an always evolving public conversation.

We talked about "United Breaks Guitars" in chapter 1. More recently, Kit Kat, long known as the chocolate bar for taking breaks, became known as something else—the chocolate bar that kills orangutans. Greenpeace had posted a delightful video to YouTube that began in the style of a typical Kit Kat ad—office workers suffering late-afternoon torpor and reaching for a sugary pick-me-up. Instead of biting into delicious chocolate wafers, though, one office drone breaks himself off a piece of orangutan finger, complete with gushing blood. Greenpeace asserted that Kit Kat parent Nestlé was using non-sustainable palm oil in the making of the candy, causing the destruction of orang habitat. The ad was followed by a takeover of Kit Kat's fan page on Facebook—with hundreds of users protesting Nestlé's practices by posting comments and by changing their Facebook photos to a doctored Kit Kat logo that spelled out the word "Killer." Major media outlets picked up the story. Now, if you are a person who is inclined to care about things like orangutans and rainforests, is any amount of perky, jingly advertising going to convince you to have a Kit Kat break?

Around the same time, Southwest Airlines was in social media meltdown too after bumping a passenger from a flight for being overweight. That passenger happened to be filmmaker Kevin Smith, an avid Twitterer with a large following. PR chaos ensued.

This isn't Bill Bernbach's media landscape anymore. That gives you, the copywriter, an incredible opportunity to push brand narrative to interactive, dynamic places it's never been before, to actually create something that generates its own audience, but it also means that many of the rules of the past—while exceedingly worthy of study—are insufficient alone to guide the modern copywriter.

In the 2006 update of *The Copywriter's Handbook,* Robert Bly asks, "Has the internet changed copywriting?" His answer is, more or less, "no." He says: "The major event that has taken place since the publication of the first edition of *The Copywriter's Handbook* is the rise of the internet as a marketing medium and channel of commerce," and goes on to say that the changes brought about by the internet have been "minor, but important" and include a reduction in consumers' attention span and more information overload.

Respectfully, this is incorrect, or at least incomplete. First, the internet cannot be viewed as simply another channel. The internet has been a much more sweeping instrument of change; as one digital agency founder has said, "digital is how you live your life." It has massively reorganized the way businesses work and interact with consumers, the way people interact with each other. If you think of digital as just another kind of advertising, you are missing almost all of its potential.

John Caples is another copywriting legend; he wrote the 1926 ad "They Laughed When I Sat Down at the Piano. But When I Started to Play . . . ," and a popular book called *Tested Advertising Methods.*

Unsurprisingly, he believed there was a science to writing ads. He believed that the headline was paramount and spent no fewer than four chapters of his book outlining exactly how to write those bank-making headlines (for example: use words that have an announcement quality, use the second person). If you're writing a headline, you may wish to embrace Caples's wisdom. But today some copywriters will never write what we've known as a headline outside of an advertising class. And good luck finding a product with a real Reevesian USP in our highly commoditized world.

That doesn't mean that the lessons of Reeves's or Caples's aren't valuable; in fact many of our creative forebears' principles are remarkably enduring. There is more to consider, though.

The following chapters will present some additional insight into copywriting now, some general, some specific to campaigns created in the last several years, much of it shared by the leading lights in today's digital, fragmented marketing world. But here are a few guiding principles, from past and future ad masters, to provide some context and maybe a framework for the discussion. These are some of the basic things informing the copywriter's work.

SELLING

Every ad wizard and copywriting how-to has said it: your job is to sell things. They may have differed in their methods, but Bernbach, Reeves, Burnett, Caples and every great copywriter before and after agreed on and was driven by this most basic goal. It sounds silly to say it, but this point seems to elude many copywriters. You have to be genuinely motivated by selling, by making a difference in the business of whomever you're writing for. Your methods may look mad or they may be purely scientific, your final product may be entertaining or informational, but every word, every idea should be in the service of the client's goals (which just might, given the nature of the corporate landscape today, include doing good for the planet, too).

If you just want to write stories for art's sake, be a novelist or a screenwriter or some other kind of writer. The job of the copywriter is too hard and you'll only get hurt.

As Gossage said, "The intent of a piece of copy is to project the client's identity, not the writer's."

STORY

When Ogilvy, Reeves, et al. bestrode Madison Avenue like chain-smoking colossi, it was a time of unprecedented prosperity. Americans had, relative to any previous era, more spare time, more money and more varieties of consumer goods available to buy. While the ad industry was born in the late 1800s and its principles developed by early giants like Hopkins, Caples and Albert Lasker, the art and science of advertising as we know it was really shaped in the forge of post-WWII America—with each of our mad men and women[5] bringing a new approach to selling an increasing number of products. But even in this time of plenty and parity products, it was possible to carve out an identity for an everyday product. Reeves found his M&M's USP because "it was the only candy in America that had chocolate surrounded by a sugar shell."

Today, well, just to begin with, there's way, way more stuff to sell. When there are 50 of everything, story becomes key.

In his must-read 2005 book *A Whole New Mind,* Daniel Pink talked about the growing importance of right-brain-oriented, or creative, thinkers as our society evolves from its industrial and information past. While the previous era had been driven by left-brain thinking—"sequential, literal, functional, textual"—the present and future belonged to the right brain—"simultaneous, metaphorical, aesthetic, contextual." Creativity, not efficiency, he said, would be the engine of economic growth. Pink boiled it down to Asia, Abundance and Automation. First, Americans have a ridiculous surfeit of things. Consider: the relatively young storage industry is worth $17 billion, more than the movie industry; Americans spend more money on garbage bags—on throwing shit away—than 90 other countries on Earth spend on *everything.* Next, an increasing number of left-brain jobs can and will go overseas and will be automated.

Pink proposed that "high concept"—the ability to detect patterns and create narratives—and "high touch"—the capacity to understand human interaction, to seek and convey meaning—were now prized attributes, that things like story, symphony, design and play are no longer the exclusive province of that tiny demographic known as "artists," but are marketable skill sets.[6]

This ability to synthesize and add meaning is particularly important now, as corporate social responsibility isn't just something for green natives like Patagonia and Seventh Generation. It is now part of the marketing order, and every corporate giant, from Walmart to P&G to GE is directly motivated financially to do, or appear to do, some version of the right thing.

Stories are simply one of the core mechanisms people use to interpret the world. In *The Big Short*, Michael Lewis's fantastic book about the 2009 meltdown of the financial industry, one of the central characters, a financial savant and one of the few people on the planet who really understood and anticipated the impossibly complex subprime mortgage fiasco tells a prospective hire, "I think in stories. I need help with numbers."[7] For copywriters, storytelling—in whatever format or media—is key to creating a meaningful brand identity.

Today, as an easy shorthand, and for lack of an accepted expression for what creative people in the ad industry actually do, most practitioners of advertising—or whatever you want to call it—say that they are brand storytellers. You may or may not choose to adopt that label. It doesn't really matter. But as a copywriter of any description, you are charged with telling a brand story, and that story may find expression in an almost infinite number of ways. This does not mean creating a narrative arc with a certain number of acts, though in the age of branded content, it may literally mean that. It might be as simple as "It is Spring and I am Blind." Or "They Laughed When I Sat Down to Play . . ."

The most classic, obvious examples of brand storytelling are, of course, TV commercials. Especially those TV spots that are, well, stories. The classic Guinness "Good Things Come to Those Who Wait" and Stella Artois's "Reassuringly Expensive" epics, or Got Milk's "Aaron Burr." Those are classic ad stories. But they only describe a small fraction of the kinds of stories copywriters tell.

One of the challenges of today's copywriter is telling a story across multiple platforms, and involving the consumer in that story.

One of the more interesting and involved kinds of story unfolds in alternate reality games, an example of what University of Southern California professor and media scholar Henry Jenkins calls transmedia storytelling. The campaign for Warner Bros.' *The Dark Knight* blockbuster was a staggeringly complex narrative that played out over several web sites, mobile phones, user-generated video, street mobs and scavenger hunts, mail, even skywriting. The campaign, which won the Cyber Grand Prix at Cannes in 2009 drew in 10 million

unique players. The film ended up having the highest opening weekend box office ever, with ticket sales of $158.3 million, and went on
to become the third highest grossing film of all time.[8]

When *The Simpsons Movie* hit theaters in 2007, it was supported by
a sweeping campaign that included a site where people could make
themselves into Simpsons-esque characters; the physical transformation of 12 real 7–11 stores into Kwik-E Marts, complete with products;
the rechristening of Jet Blue into the Official Airline of Springfield, with
guest appearances by Monty Burns on Jetblue.com; a partnership with
Vans for Simpsons-themed shoes and many other elements.

On the other hand, one of the most iconic brand stories was the
simple image of a rugged cowboy riding the range and enjoying a
smoke. The "Marlboro Man" was the creation of Leo Burnett, who
believed in the "inherent drama" of every product.

Whatever medium you end up writing for, you are creating something that takes a brand truth and makes a reader or viewer or
passerby care about it, makes it mean something in the impossibly
complicated scheme of her life.

"I think, in general, people don't buy products, they buy stories,"
says Ty Montague, former chief creative officer at JWT North America
and now founder of start-up shop Co:.. Montague is a writer by trade;
as a creative director at BBH and Wieden + Kennedy and now JWT, he
has spearheaded some innovative brand storytelling initiatives.

> All of us have our own personal narrative, the story of me. We tell
> the story of me through all the choices we make in our life; the per-
> son we choose, the schools we go to, as well as the products we buy.

COPYWRITER'S TIP

AVOID MARKETING SPEAK

You will be in situations that seem to demand using "concept" and "plus" as
verbs in the course of your job. Everyone does it. It's part of the deal.

Don't do it.

Also, don't use the words learnings. You might not realize it right away,
but slowly, inexorably, your soul will start dying.

The car, the house, the clothes—all these things advance the narrative of me. In that sense very clearly defining the story of the product and the brand is important. That allows people to identify and curate that brand. If you don't have a clearly defined story, people don't know what to do with you, how to use your brand to advance their personal narrative. At certain times, people were always looking for functional advantages, a unique selling proposition. A few products have that, they have functional superiority. But I think Rosser would have struggled to find the USP between Coke and Pepsi. There are ten of everything. Today it's about figuring out the story of your thing. Successful brands have that story built right into the design of the thing.

DESIGN

And that brings us to design. No, it's not just for art directors.

Design should inform everything a copywriter does; it should be the narrative fount from which all communication flows.

Reeves and Bernbach and the visionaries before and after them had a few things in common. A fondness for tobacco, hats and a nice Canadian Club at midday, yes, but more importantly, they all agreed on the root of any great copywriting: the product.

"The most important element in success in ad writing," said Bernbach, "is the product itself. . . . That's why we as an agency work so closely with the client on his product—looking for improvements, looking for ways to make people want it, looking for changes in the product. Because when you have that, you are giving the people something that they can't get elsewhere. And that is fundamentally what sells."[9]

Hall of famer Mary Wells Lawrence understood the power of product and design when she undertook her famous rebranding of Braniff Airlines, enlisting artist Alexander Calder to give the planes a "Flying Colors" paint job and designer Emilio Pucci to create flight attendants' uniforms.

Consider these two big statements:

"Procter & Gamble, Colgate, Bristol-Myers . . . all the big companies realized that a copywriter is almost helpless unless they build the idea into the product."

"In all our years of doing [advertising], we've found . . . that the product is always the most powerful brand-building and marketing tool."

The first quote is from Mr. McBoring USP Pants himself, Rosser Reeves. The second quote is from the book *Baked In,* written by Alex Bogusky and John Winsor, then heads of Crispin Porter + Bogusky. On the surface, the wildly creative award hog Bogusky is as philosophically removed from Reeves and his ilk as is possible. Below the surface, as always, things aren't nearly so black and white.

Brands are at their best when product and communications share a narrative, when the product, and the whole brand experience, are created through an insight-driven marketing process. This doesn't happen often—the list of marketers with a fully integrated design/marketing/advertising approach is small and begins with Apple.

But even if you're not in an agency that is literally doing product design, or working for Apple, design should be part of your thought process.

There are many ways design informs the copywriter's work. Copywriters who work in the digital realm (and this describes a growing percentage of writers, in any kind of agency) are working with technologists and are involved with interaction design and user experience design—the way a person experiences a site or other interactive system.

And then there's data—again, something that, on the surface, seems completely divorced from the world of a writer. It's not. Data is becoming a vastly more important part of the brand landscape, with more and more internal and external communications involving information visualization—taking a fathomless pool of data and creating a visually compelling representation of it—a graphical data narrative, if you like.

If storytelling is the essential job of the copywriter, design is the starting point of the story; design can inform how a story plays out and how a brand touches people at every stage in their interaction with it.

POP CULTURE

The best copywriters of the past shared another trait that is indispensable to the modern copywriter: the ability to make their words transcend the media buy and become a part of pop culture.

When Caples wrote "They Laughed When I Sat Down . . . ," his intention was to sell piano lessons, period. But that ad took on a cultural life of its own. The intro to *Tested Advertising Methods* notes, "Vaudeville comedians made jokes about it with such knee-slappers as 'They Laughed When I Sat Down at the Piano. Someone had stolen the stool.' Newspaper columnists lampooned it. Other copywriters 'borrowed' from it, copied it, paraphrased it."

The greatest ad writing has been similarly adopted in the wider cultural world—think M&Ms' "Melts in Your Mouth" and 50 Cent, think "Where's the Beef," "Wassup," the Geico cavemen, and think every time CNN or *Good Morning America* or HuffPo talks about a brand campaign today, or every time a blogger embeds a brand video.

Even when creating an ad supported by paid media, the goal is the same—having your message proactively talked about and shared by people. Wieden + Kennedy Portland recently created a TV spot for Old Spice in which ex-football player Isaiah Mustafa delivers an over-the top-performance as "The Man Your Man Could Smell Like." The spot was an instant hit with ad types—it went on to win the Film Grand Prix at Cannes in 2010—but it also become a viral sensation, racking up 6 million online views in the month after its TV debut, countless YouTube tributes, with one couple creating a rendition of the ad's dialog to the tune of John Denver's "You Fill Up My Senses," and a media phenomenon that a PR person could only dream about, with Mustafa appearing on the *Ellen DeGeneres Show, Oprah, Today, The Early Show* and *Good Morning America* in the space of a month (more on Old Spice in chapter 7).

In industry parlance, it's earned media.

"The job of the copywriter has become: can you write a great press release," says Cripin Porter + Bogusky chief creative officer Rob Reilly. "Meaning, is your idea a big enough idea that the mainstream press would write about it? Would it be something that the *New York Times* would write about? Here, a copywriter has to articulate the idea in a press release; that's how the idea starts."

Yes, the goal of your work is clear (see: Selling). But you may also want to disregard the notion of advertising altogether. You don't have to think of what you're doing as strictly writing ads. Live in the real world. Make real things that real human beings care about and want to interact with.

Once again, Gossage's words resonate: "The fact of the matter is that nobody reads ads. People read what interests them, and sometimes it's an ad."

CONVERSATION

In the real world, people have conversations.

Conversation has been one of marketing's big buzz words over the past several years and as such, like many things that are discussed ad nauseam in the marketing world, has been drained of some of its meaning.

But the idea is simple, and important. If the past was about one-way messages and the Big Ass Campaign that took months to create, ran for six weeks, then ended, the current environment calls for a more nimble, responsive, ongoing kind of communication.

New forms of storytelling make a campaign "a living thing that requires ongoing curation and involvement, on the part of storytellers and participants," says Montague.

Copywriting, in this context, is more important than it ever was, says Leo Premutico, former ECD of Saatchi & Saatchi New York, who went on to form the agency Johannes Leonardo with partner Jan Jacobs. "Especially as we have the chance to react and adjust to that conversation taking place. As brands figure out ways to become part of their consumers' lives, rather than just pay media dollars to distribute messages, the biggest and most powerful ideas allow for entertainment, and this is where the job of the writer has changed in my mind. They need to be flexible, to write for different formats, to be able to react quickly and to create something that people can latch onto."

Susan Credle, chief creative officer of Leo Burnett USA says one of her most consistent directives to the creatives she works with is to think beyond the ad to the ongoing idea. "One of the things I say over and over to the creatives I work with, especially people who have come up on TV spots, is to ask not just, is this ad funny, will it get viewed, but am I setting up an idea that will have a life of its own," says Credle. "If I'm working in a different channel is this an idea that I can play with, can a social media idea draft off of it, can PR be a part of it, etc. We're starting to test how big the ideas can be, how long they can go and where they can go. I don't want to spend money on advertising, I want to invest money in something. When I spend money on an ad campaign, it means, when that campaign is finished running, that's it, there's nothing else. I think when you have an idea that you're investing in, you can stop spending and through earned media, it still has a life. There isn't a finality to it, there is an ongoing story."

BERNBACH'S ENDURING RULE

We'll talk about examples of all of the above in the subsequent chapters. But one note to end this discussion of the fundamentals.

Earlier, we mentioned an uncomfortable truth in passing. It's painful but necessary to revisit it. We mentioned Head On! and Guinness "Surfer" in the same sentence and the fact that, strictly speaking, both ads worked; both ads moved the sales needles for the brands involved.

We could say that in this world of choice and control, a pure meritocracy has emerged. That since people are no longer passive consumers of whatever Big Media serves up, they will demand better. That since the viewing public is a more active participant in the media world, only the best content will rise to the top. We could say that, but it would, of course, be fantasy.

If the new consumer control world meant a glorious Eden of better content, we wouldn't have renewed seasons of *Keeping Up with the Kardashians* and *Real Housewives of Oh My God It's Like Watching Paint Dry Only the Paint Is Hateful, Vapid and Over-tanned.*

If this book has a philosophical point of view, it's that you the copywriter are responsible for putting things into the world, and those things should be useful, entertaining or beautiful, or all of those things. They should make people feel better, not worse, about themselves, the brand involved and living in the world in general. Given all the changes in the media environment and the new opportunities for writers we discuss in this book, one thing becomes clear—brand messages are becoming more ubiquitous, more integrated into every part of a person's life. That's a potentially horrible thought.

And here is where the examples of Bernbach and Gossage are most important. In fact, we'll allow Bernbach the final word on copywriting fundamentals: "All of us who professionally use the mass media are the shapers of society. We can vulgarize that society. We can brutalize it. Or we can help lift it onto a higher level."

CHAPTER 3

THE STORYTELLERS

If we measure advertising's evolution with brand campaigns, there are several that warrant mention as epochal milestones that marked the forward movement of an industry. They helped accelerate the pace of change as they took the new realities of consumer behavior and built them into brand ideas. They put the ad business on notice. And they expanded the job description of the copywriter.

No conversation about brand-creativity milestones in the modern era can begin without a discussion of BMW Films.

The campaign, called "The Hire" and created out of Fallon Minneapolis, was simple by today's standards—a series of lavishly produced films distributed primarily on a dedicated web site (this, distressingly, remained the digital strategy of many marketers for many years afterward). It was, in many ways, an old idea, having a brand sponsor entertainment content. However, it's hard to overestimate the impact of BMW Films on the brand landscape and, directly and indirectly, on the evolution of the copywriter's job.

The campaign launched in April 2001. Cinema trailers and TV spots drove viewers to BMWFilms.com, which housed a series of slick films. A few things made this campaign distinctive at the time. First, these were not just big online car ads. They were six- to ten-minute pieces of cinema. And, unlike most commercials, which star, well, commercial actors, this campaign featured a film star who was on the rise in Hollywood—the categorically dreamy Clive Owen—as the central character, "The Driver." Owen's supporting cast over the eight films included name actors, such as Forest Whitaker, Mickey Rourke, Don Cheadle and other cultural icons. In one film, *Star,* Madonna, stretched her acting muscles playing a diva with a bad attitude; another, *Beat the Devil,* featured James Brown battling for his soul against a spandex-clad Satan portrayed by Gary Oldman, with Marilyn Manson in cameo. And these films had accomplished feature directors attached—John Frankenheimer, Wong Kar-Wai, Ang Lee, Guy Ritchie and Tony Scott were among the auteurs who directed the first and second series in the campaign. This wasn't web film as it would come to be known in the early YouTube era—lo-fi, low budget, DIY, reality-leaning. BMW Films took the entire big-budget ethic of the heyday of TV spots and stepped on the gas—the films were narrative driven, cinematic, and, at an estimated $15 million for the series, expensive.[1]

Fallon had been charged with creating a new campaign for BMW—it was a rare assignment that didn't revolve around the launch of a new model; rather, Fallon's mandate was to create a Big Brand Campaign. The Fallon creative team, led by then-associate creative director Bruce Bildsten, copywriter/group creative director Joe Sweet and art director David Carter working under Fallon president and executive creative director David Lubars, presented BMW some TV spot–driven campaign ideas; but the automaker's marketing team, fronted by Jim McDowell, VP marketing, North America, wasn't satisfied. And so, Fallon was given a directive that surely inspired equal parts excitement and terror: impress us. The client "sent us an inspiring letter," says Bildsten. "They were asking for a brand campaign but they were asking for something more. They said, we want you to take off the gloves. Come back with something to blow us away."

The team's inspiration for the ultimate driving idea came from a few sources. A short time before, Sweet and Carter had worked with film director Tim Burton on a Timex campaign and came away impressed by the director's creative process and prodigious talent. But more important was what the creatives had learned about BMW's core customer. The BMW buyer was, typically, a mid-40s male with a median income of about $150,000.[2] Something else stood out about the automaker's fortunate customer base—85 percent of them used the internet for research before buying their car, which, at the turn of the century, wasn't yet a matter of course.

Here we see the beginnings of the internet's impact on traditional advertising. Yes, the web was adding to media fragmentation and making it harder to reach certain people through TV and print. But more to the point, it was starting to change consumer behavior; it was becoming the locus of brand information, opinion sharing, decision making.

Looking back, one might note that the history of automotive advertising is peppered with creative milestones; it's such a big and lucrative category that it has at times yielded remarkable feats of creativity and experimentation. VW, Saturn, BMW, Mini, Fiat—some of the work done for these brands made ad and sales history. But note also that between VW "Think Small" and BMW Films, the history of car advertising was a history of TV spots. And not all the spots were made of the same iconoclastic magic as Think Small. If you're over 20, you're aware that automotive advertising has also been a dismal slurry of sheet metal, winding roads and salt flats. Generally, car makers and their agencies seemed altogether satisfied creating and airing an indistinguishable series of loving shots of shiny cars driving a coastal highway or spinning around in the desert, with the occasional sexy lady thrown in.

BMW Films marked a turning point. Fallon's idea was to create content that people would go out of their way to watch. Instead of, as Gossage put it, riding on someone else's audience, they were creating their own audience. Instead of an interruption, BMW Films was a destination. The campaign appealed to potential BMW buyers where they lived with a narrative experience that was in keeping with the BMW brand. This wasn't the first web film or web ad by any means. Even in 2001, four years before the dawn of YouTube, there was a small assortment of web channels that hosted mainly short, comedic content, the most popular being Atom Films. But BMW Films was the first big-ticket, cinematic piece of brand content that gained public attention.

COPYWRITERS AS SCREENWRITERS

Bildsten, Carter and Sweet had initially taken their idea for a web film to director David Fincher. The director, who was known for his visually innovative commercials and music videos as well as features like

Fight Club, was already committed to his next film, *Panic Room,* but he was interested in the project, so he signed on as an executive producer and exercised significant creative influence over the project. Fallon's original concept was to do one long film in several segments; it was Fincher's idea to do a series of separate films.

Fincher also felt that it would take experienced screenwriters to do justice to the films, and, as Bildsten recalls, there was a writers' strike underway in Hollywood at the time, so A-list talent was available. Bildsten says that Sweet and Carter also started writing scripts themselves. "They surprised Fincher and the client," says Bildsten. "We had heavyweight screen writers, and Joe and David and [Fallon copywriter] Greg Hahn on the second batch of films wrote scripts that were just as good if not better."

A total of eight films were released: Season 1, produced out of Fincher and producer Steve Golin's company, Anonymous Content, consisted of *Ambush* by John Frankenheimer, *The Follow* by Wong Kar-Wai, *Chosen* by Ang Lee, *Star* by Guy Ritchie and *Powder Keg* by Alejandro González Iñárritu; Season 2, produced with Ridley Scott's RSA Films, comprised *Hostage* by John Woo, *Ticker* by Joe Carnahan and *Beat the Devil* by Tony Scott.

In each film, The Driver is hired as a fixer for someone in need, and he employs his driving skill, his range of high-performance BMWs and various other smooth spy-like faculties to solve problems. The storylines and tone of the films vary from dramatic to violent to comedic, but they all revolve around Owen expertly putting a range of gorgeous Bavarian motor vehicles through their paces. There was no mention of the brand outside of the closing credits' copyright and a reminder from BMW to always wear a seatbelt. None was necessary. The cars—and the brand's central performance message—were always front and center, but always in the context of a compelling story.

The films were a creative collaboration between agency and production company, with the directors and agency writers sharing credit for the stories and scripts. Andrew Kevin Walker, a screenwriter with credits including *Seven* and *Sleepy Hollow,* wrote *Ambush* and *The Follow.* The rest of the films were written in whole or in part by Sweet, Carter and Hahn.

Sweet, the writer who started it all and who wrote two of the films, sadly died in late 2002 of a heart ailment. He was 43. Carter was an art

COPYWRITER'S TIP

DON'T FORGET THE STORY

Many creatives have talked about the importance of storytelling in many different ways. Here's how Conway Williamson, executive creative director of Saatchi & Saatchi New York sums up the storytelling imperative:

"If you can't tell a story you ain't shit."

director at the time but, Bildsten says, he trained himself to be a scriptwriter; he wrote *Chosen* and co-wrote *Beat the Devil, Powder Keg* and *Hostage*. "He was an early example of someone who spread their wings and said, I'm not just going to leave this to my writing partner. David and the other agency writers read every book on screenwriting to try and learn as much as possible about the craft. Which is another lesson from this—never stop learning just because you're working in a great agency and your ad school days are long past."

Fallon copywriter Hahn, who had writing credits on *Hostage* and *Beat the Devil*, was brought in for the second round of films. "When I came in, David Carter in particular wanted to take more of a hand in writing. I came in and David and I worked for months writing scripts and stuff before we sent them out to directors."

The process of writing for mini-features was indeed different from working on 30-second commercials, both in terms of the specific nature of BMW Films, which saw big-name directors take more control over the idea and the scripts, and generally in terms of writing for the longer format.

"It was an eye-opening experience," says Hahn. "It made me realize how good we have it in advertising as writers—you have a lot of control. In commercials, the writer is charged with seeing the idea all the way through. But if you're talking about films and the Hollywood model, once you've written a script, they don't want your input after that. It is a director and producer medium. And rightly so. You realize that people are going to click a John Woo film and not a Greg Hahn film. They cast and they edited it; on set you were there watching, whereas on a commercial shoot I work closely with the directors."

The model for BMW Films was to hire big directorial talent and give the directors control to see through their vision of the idea—a rarity in the ad world, where creatives and, yes, even clients will often weigh in on executional choices throughout the process.

But for Hahn and the other writers, writing what were essentially short films represented a more fundamental new challenge. "At first it seemed kind of daunting, but in the end it was kind of freeing," says Hahn. "One of the biggest challenges of spots is that you only have 30 seconds to play with; it's an exercise in whittling down. On the other side of that, with a film, you have to make sure there is more than one idea there—it has to have scenes that link to each other and carry out an entire story. Spots are very concentrated—it's one scene, it's usually a gag that's played out. This was about creating movement and scenes. You have to consider it all leading to the end moment."

Given the limited supply of good online short content at the time, Hahn says he took his cues from short stories and watching feature films and dissecting scenes, especially nonlinear films, like *Pulp Fiction.* "You think of it like a short story—like an O'Henry story. It's all about building to one single moment. In these shorts it's all about what the last thing people see and walk away with."

With The Driver so key to the narrative, the writers were also charged with creating that character, complete with back story, before cameras started rolling. Who was this man, where did he come from, what drove him? If audiences are going to be interacting with a story over longer stretches of time, the characters and stories require more of a framework to support that richer, more complex narrative. This is one major addition to the copywriter's job in the post-2000 era—in the manner of screenwriters, copywriters now spend more of their time as story architects before any dialog is written or any frame or pixel produced. We'll come back to this in discussions of campaigns in the following pages—the increasing importance of behind-the-scenes writing, of back story, guidelines and narrative underpinnings.

A TITANIUM MOMENT IN ADVERTISING

Did the Fallon team know at the time that they were creating ad history? Bildsten says that once the idea was sold to BMW's senior marketers, everyone immediately saw its potential. Bildsten recalls standing with BMW CEO Tom Purvis at a Formula One race after Purvis had learned about the campaign. "He said it's either going to be an incredible success that people will talk about for years or no one will pay any attention," says Bildsten.

It was to BMW's credit that it was the former. It should be noted that media innovation aside, what made BMW Films great was, well, the great films. Watch them now—they stand the test of time. They're simply compelling entertainment. After the client approved the scripts—scripts that were orders of magnitude edgier than any car ad: how many spots have you seen that feature themes of domestic violence and narco war?—the directors were given free rein to weave their storytelling magic. It's surprising how infrequently this actually happens. In a depressingly typical scenario, advertisers will enlist talented people to work on ad projects and then proceed to tell them how to do their jobs.

It's an exceedingly rare client that takes risks and trusts its agency and production partners to deliver on their creative promises. Many of the landmark creative campaigns featured in these pages start, as we've noted, with a great product and a marketer who understands what the product and the brand stand for and how to extend the brand story through any communications platform.

They also start with a marketer who understands that the goal is not to make an ad—it's to make something worthwhile that earns audience attention and conveys a brand truth.

BMW Films, like many groundbreaking campaigns before and after it, drew nay-saying along with praise. The criticism tended to fall into the "Where's the ad?"/"What does this have to do with selling cars?" column.

There have been experiments in branding that have consisted essentially of an interesting film or other creation with an arbitrary brand logo slapped on at the end and that have deserved such criticism.

And this is where skilled creatives come in. The job isn't to create your version of art. That's not to say there isn't art in creating great brand content and experiences, or that someone might not look at your creation and see art. But art, as the man said, is useless. Your art has a very specific job to do.

BMW Films is an example of a brand campaign that walked this line successfully, that offered an entertainment experience that earned an audience and that was an effective brand story. There have been many more.

Another factor in BMW Films' success was the agency's approach to marketing the films. Bildsten says the agency followed a "whisper to a shout" strategy, seeding the films online with movie critics and other influential people before publicly trumpeting the campaign. The agency also made a point of playing down its own involvement—the name Fallon wasn't the dominant presence in the films' credits, which focused instead on the big-name directors and stars. "So it felt more like BMW's contribution to the arts rather than a marketing effort," says Bildsten. "In many ways it was—it was a more artistic venture than most marketing efforts. But there was no mistake about the brand behind the films. We were careful about that. We wanted to be honest that BMW is behind this thing yet still presenting it as pure entertainment."

It all worked spectacularly well, as word spread among film fans online and culminated in major press coverage—one of the earliest and most prominent stories was by Richard Corliss of *Time* magazine.

In the first phase of the campaign, the films were viewed 10 million times on BMWFilms.com. Ninety-four percent of the 2 million people who registered on BMWFilms.com passed on the films to others. In the wake of the campaign, visits to dealerships increased, awareness of the brand increased among a younger demographic, and, most important, BMW sold 213,127 cars in 2001, up 12 percent from the previous year.[3]

And while they knew they had created something exceptional, the creatives associated with BMW Films could not have known what a gigantic impact their films would have on the ad industry. The campaign immediately reflected and hastened the changes that were beginning to remake advertising. Out of the box, BMW Films became the poster campaign for branded content and for the shift to internet distribution. The Hire was the proto "nontraditional" campaign. For years—in fact right up to today—it has been discussed and dissected by the ad industry as a signifier of changing times. It was the campaign that inspired an uninspiring trend among marketers, who, upon launching a new campaign, would simply say to their agency "Give me one of those." And of course the imitators followed.

The award shows even had to create new categories for it; at the 2002 Cannes ad festival, BMW Films was shut out of the film awards as it didn't fit the show's categorical criteria. The following year, Dan Wieden, founder of Wieden + Kennedy, served as the chairman of the film jury at the Cannes ad festival and created a new award category: the Titanium Lion. The new prize, he said, was for work "in any category, or any combination of categories, that causes the industry to stop in its tracks and reconsider the way forward" and was a nod to BMW Films' impact on the industry.

The campaign ushered in a new era of branded content, product placement and new relationships between entertainment and advertising players. In many ways this harked back to the earliest days of TV, when advertisers sponsored programming rather than paying for 30-second ad breaks.

Since Fallon's breakthrough, several automakers, including BMW subsidiary MINI, have launched new campaigns and models with little to no TV advertising; they use a wider and wider array of means of not only telling stories, but gathering and interpreting data, and they use technology to link the driving experience with the brand message. In 2008, European automaker Fiat and digital agency AKQA London created something called eco:Drive. The initiative was based around an application designed to monitor driving data—acceleration, deceleration, fuel consumption, "driving style"—that could be transferred from car to computer via USB stick and what Fiat called "Blue&Me" technology. In October 2009, VW announced that it wouldn't even bother with the web, much less with TV. VW would base its entire campaign for the new model GTI on an iPhone app.

Bildsten went on to start his own shop, Brew Creative in Minneapolis. Carter and Hahn followed Fallon president David Lubars to BBDO. As executive creative director, Hahn authored another high-profile branded content initiative for HBO in 2008 called "Voyeur," which saw him and Carter, along with creative director/art director Mike Smith, stretching their writing skills once again. The campaign for the high-end cable channel allowed viewers to seemingly peep into an apartment building and observe the freaky goings on therein. The campaign launched with a giant outdoor spectacle—an HD projection on a building on New York's Lower East Side that made it appear to street viewers that they were looking into eight apartments. Web viewers could witness an interactive version of the spectacle online. The main film component, directed by RSA's Jake Scott, required a feat of choreographed storytelling—Hahn and team had to create a story for each of the eight apartments that would stand alone and yet play out in a precise manner so as to create an intertwining narrative.

"It was different from any other writing I've done," says Hahn. "There were no cuts, and there was only one take, with no device of zooming in to highlight part of the story, and you couldn't rely on dialog to tell the story. It all had to be played out as if you were watching across the street and in a way that kept your attention as well."

For the main film, everything had to be scripted so that the timing of the individual stories would match up, as some of the stories were related. And, once again, much of the heavy lifting for the writer lay in creating the back story for the characters on which the intertwining narratives could rest. "Once we got the scenarios down of who is in those rooms we wrote back stories for those people—what their relationships were to each other, how they got there, etc. It was pages and pages for each person. We didn't script it out second by second, we wrote out a little play for each floor and the actors would rehearse for weeks. They knew the characters and the timing and the basic story but the rest was up to them to pantomime their way through. It was interesting, the scripts were pretty short; more important were the back stories. They had to be intuitive to the actors by the time we got to rolling film."

The bigger picture creative challenge was conceiving an idea that was worthy of HBO—the king of cable storytellers. "HBO is known for being great storytellers," says Hahn. "You could write lines and spots that say how HBO is a great storyteller, but we wanted to do something that embodied that. We wanted to create a different way to tell a story that was interesting to watch in itself and reflected on the brand that way."

AN ALTERNATE AD REALITY

The mandate to create a compelling story that represents a brand's ethos and invites interaction and sharing rather than dictating a message would carry over into many of the other breakthrough story-driven campaigns in this ad era.

A few years after Fallon took the gloves off and delivered the knockout that was BMW Films, video game enthusiasts started seeing some alarming posts on game-site discussion boards. It seemed that SEGA had gone too far with its latest title, and one beta tester was out to prove that the game company was literally making him crazy.

What gamers didn't know, though many suspected, was that the beta tester, "Beta 7," wasn't real. He was the creation of agency Wieden + Kennedy New York, and he was part of a new campaign for SEGA's ESPN NFL Football 2K4 game. Though calling Beta 7 a campaign seems wrong. As much as creating a campaign, the agency had planted the seeds of a story that unfolded over four months in ways that even they couldn't predict at the outset.

The Wieden team, led by then–creative directors Ty Montague and Todd Waterbury and including copywriter Bobby Hershfield and art director Rob Rasmussen, was charged with creating an impact in the gaming community that was disproportionate to the small budget for the new title. SEGA was by far the underdog in a game category owned by EA Sports juggernaut Madden Football, which drastically outsold and outspent SEGA.

Again, even with some stellar commercials, the blunt instrument of TV wasn't likely to create the desired reaction among the game's target audience. If BMW's midlife-crisis demographic was spending enough time online to warrant a web-based campaign, you can imagine the difficulty of reaching avid male gamers aged 12–24 through any traditional media.

Before the SEGA brief came along, Montague had been interested in an unusual 2001 campaign for Steven Spielberg's feature *Artificial Intelligence: AI*. The campaign, called "The Beast," drew audiences into a story via a number of cryptic clues, tiny threads that those who were paying very close attention could grab and use to unravel a narrative across a range of media. One of the main "rabbit holes" for the story came via *AI* trailers, which included a credit for one Jeanine Salla, a "Sentient Machine Therapist." Further clues, including a phone number encoded into some copy on a trailer, hinted that Salla was the key to a murder that had taken place.

By the time the story had unfolded, it involved 30 web sites, live events, TV commercials, phone calls, texts and newspaper ads. A growing community of people would discover and share story elements and slowly unravel the story together.

The game was created by a secret Microsoft team that included Sean Stewart, Jordan Weisman and Elan Lee, who would go on to form a company devoted to this kind of immersive storytelling, 42 Entertainment, about which more later.

Stewart, a novelist and a pioneer of this new art form, detailed The Beast on his blog. In the post he recalled: "In an earlier conversation, Jordan had been sitting around mulling the idea over with Elan Lee, when his phone rang. He glanced at Elan, grinning. 'Wouldn't it be cool if that was the game calling?'

"Not only would that make it cool, it would make it more real. The idea was that the fiction should jump the dike. A book you can close, a movie happens in a theater—but the Game should evade those boundaries. If our imaginary world called you on your real phone, wasn't it at least as real as the telemarketers doing the same thing? Realer, because you would have seen pictures of the imaginary people calling you. You'd know things about their childhood, their hopes and disappointments, their taste in food."[4] One of the basic premises of The Beast, said Stewart, was that "the game would never admit it was a game."

The Beast was perhaps the first brand-related example of what would come to be known as an alternate reality game (ARG), what media scholar Henry Jenkins calls transmedia storytelling. It drew 2 million "players" from around the world.

Back at Wieden, Montague chose to generate interest among gamers for the lesser-known SEGA title by focusing the campaign on the game's new "First Person Football" feature, which provided a more visceral game experience by allowing players to assume the perspective of their gridiron avatar. It's worth noting here that, even this complex, seemingly chaotic campaign was designed around a specific product attribute, a downright Reevsian USP.

The agency did create some funny TV spots that starred then-SNL cast member Tracy Morgan, but, more memorably, the team created a character and an open-ended, participatory story, an alternate reality game.

In mid-2003, an anonymous character appeared online, first in message boards on game-oriented sites. The character introduced himself as Beta 7, because, as he would relay in great detail, he was a volunteer beta tester of SEGA Football and was experiencing some troubling after effects. After testing the game at SEGA HQ, Beta 7 claimed to be experiencing bizarre blackouts, during which he would violently tackle people—presumably owing to exposure to up-close violence via First Person Football, or Crash Cam. He began documenting his blackouts on his site, beta7.com, complete with video footage, photos of his injuries and copies of his desperate letters to SEGA asking for explanation. Gaming fans started flooding his and other discussion boards with comments. The story progressed as an ostensible SEGA insider, Beta X, sent Beta 7 shredded documents as proof that the company knew of the deleterious effects of Crash Cam; he also sent him beta copies of the game. Beta 7 posted game footage to his site, prompting gamers to ask for copies of the game; nine gamers received the illicit copies and then received letters from SEGA's legal department demanding they send the games back. More story layers were added—SEGA's launch of faux-gamer site Gamer Chuck, Beta 7's hacking of SEGA's main site and redirecting traffic to his site, and so on.

Beta 7's first posts appeared online in July 2003 (though supporting material that corroborated his story dated back to March), and by the time the campaign wrapped, it had involved several blogs and sites, message boards, newspaper ads, voice mail messages, direct mail, live stunts and other elements.

The agency enlisted one of the few production partners that could claim to have significant experience in this complex form of storytelling.

Haxan Films, also known as directors Edouardo Sanchez and Daniel Myrick and producers Greg Hale and Mike Monello, were the filmmakers behind 1999's surprise mega-hit *The Blair Witch Project*. The film, considered the ultimate in horror by some and simply nauseating by others, was made for a reported $35,000 and reaped $140 million at the box office. But the filmmakers gained as much attention for the way they marketed their strange, low-budget film as for the snotty-nose close-ups and shaky panic-cam visual style that made the film such a divisive yet decisive pop-culture phenomenon.

The Haxans carried the premise of the film—a weird myth about a backwoods demon and a trio of young filmmakers who disappeared while investigating it—into the marketing of the film, playing with the boundaries between reality and the film's narrative. The campaign, which included newspaper clippings about the disappearance of the filmmakers, missing person fliers and found footage, caused cynical young consumers to question basic principles. Surely this was a ruse. Or, geez . . . was there really a Blair Witch?

Haxans Monello and Sanchez collaborated with the Wieden team and Orlando digital production company GMD Studios on Beta 7. The agency creative team of Hershfield and Rasmussen conceived the basic premise behind the campaign—the idea of a rogue beta tester who was having blackouts and was out to expose SEGA for unleashing a potentially dangerous game on the public. Monello and Sanchez took the agency's basic idea and spun it out into the four-month-long narrative that changed daily according to level of audience participation and gamer feedback.

From their office in Orlando, Monello and Sanchez and an Orlando-based writer named Jim Gunshanan spearheaded what Monello and Montague called "interactive theater," or what Montague described at the time as "improv marketing—like doing *Saturday Night Live* seven days a week."

"They wanted to express the idea that the game was so realistic that it was causing a psychotic reaction," says Monello, who now creates alternate reality games and other interactive campaigns out of Campfire, a company he formed in 2005 with Hale and Steve Wax, an executive producer who had founded production company Chelsea Films. "The story was the beta tester testing the game and having these blackouts and then working to stop SEGA—that's what the client bought. Once they bought it, it was a matter of sitting down and plotting the whole back story; it's not like the whole story can happen in real time, so we had to think through the whole story from before the campaign started to figuring out when he would go public, when would he try and attract attention to his cause. The question was, how will we tell that back story and what will we do to move the story forward." Monello says that process entailed, literally, loosely plotting out the story in a linear way on a big desk calendar. "The rest of it was, we'll see what the audience was doing in response and we'll react from there." The campaign also rested on a well-developed character—Monello and Gunshanan wrote a manifesto for Beta 7 as a guide for his behavior and reactions. Gunshanan wrote the character and met daily with Monello; the two met with Wieden creatives weekly to determine the course of the campaign.

"We were able to create a framework for experiences," says Monello. "We would get people telling the story to each other."

Monello says one of the key moments in the campaign was the point at which SEGA sent "pirated" beta copies of the game to nine gamers who were interacting with the campaign. "So you had people getting these games and then going back to their gaming communities and saying 'Oh My god, I got this.' They'd take pictures and talk about it and it created excitement around the game and where Beta 7 was going."

It would have been less interesting, says Monello, if SEGA had started out by just contacting gamers and sending them copies of its new game. "I think that this audience at that time was pretty cynical when they were approached by a company," he says. "So I think if people would have got early copies of the game from SEGA, then what those people were saying about the game would have been looked at in suspicious terms by other people. Whereas having a crazy story that framed this message of—this game is so intense that it's dangerous—by framing it that way we gave a fun context to those people who received copies of the game and they could talk about it on their own terms."

In the ensuing years, marketers and agencies would go back to the hoax-narrative well often—too often.

Monello says that Beta 7 would have unfolded very differently today. Transparency is more important today in these kinds of immersive stories. While brand campaigns still play out like scavenger hunts and enmesh people in an often shady, evolving narrative, it's unwise to leave an audience feeling duped in the end. Many ARGs made in more recent years—like 42 Entertainment's *Dark Knight* ARG, and Campfire's own *True Blood* campaign—have been up front about the company or brand involved, though the stories are no less mysterious and absorbing.

Monello also says that since Beta 7, "creatives are getting smarter about why people are interested in stories"; he also notes that the story would have unfolded in different directions with new technologies like location-aware services. But the lasting lesson from the campaign is the idea of involving an audience in a brand narrative, of having your audience willingly tell your story for you. "It's not about the platform; it's what are you doing with people and how are they behaving and how does that intersect. We use narrative to bring people into a world. We devise a story—like a beta tester who blacks out—and figure out how we can bring that story to life so people will tell that story for us, so they have a role and participate in it somehow."

When the campaign ran its course, there were 70,000 unique visitors to Beta7.com and 680,000 page views, but, more important, said Montague in a *Creativity* interview at the time, visitors spent an average of 10.5 minutes once at the site, versus the internet average of 30 seconds or less. According to GMD's reckoning, it all translated into 2.25 million media exposures to the campaign. "The facts and figures about traffic are one way to look at it," Montague told *Creativity.* "Another is what impact it had on the culture of gaming. It's harder, though more important to get at the latter. We wanted to generate buzz and controversy among the people in the hardcore gaming community, who basically decide what everyone else thinks about the game."

Says Monello, "I'm starting to see marketers consider something that's always been a reality for me—that maybe it's not the biggest audience we should be going after. If I'm trying to sell a horror story, what can I give to people who are really into horror stories that will give them a context in which to spread the story? In other words, if I know you love vampire stories and I give you something that you like, you will run out and tell your friend. But the great thing is that you will tell your friend in a way you know your friend wants to hear because you know your friend better than I do."

In 2009, Campfire created a transmedia campaign for Discovery's famous Shark Week that saw the team send jars to bloggers and reporters—jars containing, among other things, chewed, bloodied swimwear, a boat key and a newspaper clipping of the recipient's obit detailing her life and subsequent death—by shark attack. The story continued on a web site, frenziedwaters.com and went from there. James Hibberd, a blogger for *The Hollywood Reporter* duly wrote about the strange gift, saying, "Today was the first time a network ever truly creeped me out."

Critics of ARGs have wondered just who has the inclination to pick up on arcane clues and follow the thin thread of a narrative that's purposely hidden amid the media noise we all filter daily. And a full-scale ARG is not for every marketer.

But a number of other ARGs have advanced the art of interactive storytelling while finding a substantial audience—42 also created "Why So Serious," the ARG based on the blockbuster film *The Dark Knight,* which claimed 10 million unique participants.

Quantitative data aside, the ARG approach—creating something with the feeling of being "real," rather than an ad, tantalizing people with an unusual discovery, and compelling them to share stories— is a transcendent creative imperative. That ARG spirit translates into many different kinds of brand creative, some of which we'll discuss in the next chapter.

The notion of interactive storytelling has clearly changed the job of the writer, or at least added a new layer to the basic skill set.

Montague says he's always looking for writers who have an appreciation for great storytelling, "not to the exclusion of someone who can tell a great story in 30 seconds. That's still important," he says. "But I'm also looking for people who have an appreciation for the arc of a longer story. That's becoming more and more important. And, additionally, and this is where it gets interesting, someone who has the ability to keep the overall arc of a story in their head after that story has been shattered and hidden in different places in the world."

The biggest challenge in this kind of storytelling, says Montague, is that it is truly interactive. "Once you have the whole arc of the story in your head—and you've assembled all the pieces, you're not sure which parts people will get excited about and which part people will miss or ignore. So it's like a piece of live theater in that if you see the audience is not responding or is getting bored, you have to respond and improvise on the fly to fill in the interest gaps or understanding gaps that only become evident once you release the story into the wild. Unlike traditional storytelling where you complete the thing and you put it out there, it's a living thing that requires ongoing curation and involvement on the part of storytellers and participants."

CHAPTER 4

DIGITAL IS NOT A CHANNEL

On April 7, 2004, an assortment of unsuspecting people received a link to a surprising, one might even say troubling, web site. The SubservientChicken.com home page was Googlesque in its simplicity, consisting of what appeared to be a web cam window against a black background. Visitors were met with the sight of a humanoid figure dressed in a chicken suit accessorized with a garter belt. A text box invited viewers to "Get Chicken the Way You Like it" and to enter a command. When visitors typed in whatever impromptu directive came into their heads—"Sit down," "Skip" or "Do the moonwalk"— the seemingly impossible happened. The chicken sat down, or skipped or moonwalked. The whole thing, from set decor to the grainy look of the video to the name of the site smacked of DIY web porn, by design. The first few people who were emailed or IM'd the link were relatively sophisticated media consumers. But this was a site the likes of which even they had never seen. So, they did what the site compelled them to do—they spent, on average, nearly six minutes playing with the magic chicken, and then they passed it along to everyone they knew.

The site was created by agency Crispin Porter + Bogusky and digital company The Barbarian Group, as a companion to a series of similarly themed TV spots.

The spots, it's worth noting, were excellent. Created by CP+B copywriter Bob Cianfrone and art director Mark Taylor, and directed by Rocky Morton, they were unprecedented in the annals of fast-food advertising for their shockingly dark and creepy tone. And they were promptly forgotten. The site, meanwhile, became a cultural phenomenon. Within 24 hours, SubservientChicken.com had garnered a million views; after a week, more than 20 million people had bent the chicken to their will. The site was covered endlessly in mainstream media outlets, generating an estimated 7 million broadcast impressions. By the following year, the site had drawn over 350 million views.[1]

Like BMW Films before it, Subservient Chicken embodied, in one feathery, complaisant package, another disruptive shift in how brand ideas were being created, consumed and distributed. And it helped change the game and the goals of copywriting.

A disclaimer seems appropriate here. As you can discern from the number at the top of the chapter, this is a separate chapter dealing specifically with the digital space. This chapter shouldn't exist, really. A separate chapter on digital runs counter to the philosophy espoused by leading creatives and elsewhere in this book—that the web isn't just another channel through which ads can be distributed, that writers should think first about ideas, not media-specific ads, that digital permeates everything a brand and, by extension, a writer, does.

But the changes wrought by the internet, the digital revolution, if you will, are fundamental to the role of the writer now, and, if we're being realistic, the ad landscape hasn't yet adjusted to a truly integrated model.

The rise of digital drove home the point that as ad creatives, your job isn't to create something that consumers would readily identity as "An Ad." Your job is to create engaging, entertaining or useful content or experiences on behalf of a brand. And so, we step back briefly to look at writers in the digital world and to hear from the creatives behind some of the most important "digital" work.

INDISTINGUISHABLE FROM MAGIC

If BMW Films was a landmark in the evolution of brand storytelling and branded content, Subservient Chicken similarly marked a watershed in the new era of interactive creativity. A weird watershed. But a watershed.

Both campaigns embodied the essential shift from brand messages as paid interruption to entertainment content toward brand messages as entertainment content. They were two drastically different examples of agencies creating content that audiences actively sought out, that they chose to spend time with—more time, by the way, than they had ever spent on a typical ad—and that they chose to share with others. Though both campaigns had a paid media component, both BMW Films and the Subservient Chicken web site were mainly distributed for free, virally, passed along by people who were eager to share what they'd experienced with friends. Subservient Chicken, though, represented another breakthrough or two.

First, the site was, literally, interactive. Just as the first motion pictures didn't fully exploit the medium's capabilities, but simply took the earlier visual experience of theater and placed it on film, many of the early interactive ad campaigns transposed advertising's classic narrative—or an extended version of it—to the web. TV spots became web videos, print ads became banners. It would take some time for brands to start experimenting with things that were organic to the internet, that were intrinsically interactive. In fact, the industry is still figuring this out. Subservient Chicken was a creation of the internet, of the digital age. It was a brand experience that exploited the particular properties of the medium and the behavior it allowed.

Second, the Subservient Chicken web site made it abundantly clear that agencies, copywriters and other creative thinkers responsible for creating campaigns had to have some understanding of technology, or had to work very closely with someone who did.

Many ad veterans are fond of repeating the mantra that regardless of the vast changes in media consumption and technology, an idea is an idea. The basics don't change. Well, yes and no.

As we'll explore here, the Subservient Chicken site was simple, its core idea classic. When CP+B took over the account in 2004, Burger King was struggling, both sales-wise and in terms of establishing any kind of meaningful identity through its communications. As Burger King CMO Russ Klein told *Advertising Age* at the time, "We were a brand that suffered from a lack of emotional attachment." CP+B immediately resurrected the chain's legacy tag line, "Have it Your Way." It was a perfect positioning for the digital era—Burger King became the brand for customization, for consumer control.

One of CP+B's early assignments was promoting the burger chain's Tender Crisp Chicken Sandwich. The agency's central idea for the chicken push sprung from the Have it Your Way theme: Chicken the Way You Like It. The agency could, and did, produce some TV commercials, and it could have made a web site on which to run those commercials and dispense other information around the sandwich.

But, how do you make the leap from those standard ad ideas to the idea of—"Hey, let's allow people to literally get chicken to do whatever they say?" You can only get there by knowing how consumers are behaving in the real world and by knowing what's possible from a technological standpoint. And you can only know those things by employing or working with people who care about those things.

Subservient Chicken's success was due in no small part to the fact that it blew people's minds. Though fun and frivolous, it embodied sci fi author and futurist Arthur C. Clarke's famed tenet: "Any sufficiently advanced technology is indistinguishable from magic." To the casual observer, it was sort of magic. How else could a chicken be responding to your commands over the internet??

In the earlier days of the internet, many traditional agencies considered the whole digital advertising thing an unglamorous afterthought. Other traditional agencies—like CP+B—and, of course, digital-native agencies embraced it as a core discipline. By the early 00s, they were reaping the benefits of their investment in digital as marketers began directing more of their money and attention toward interactive, and the creative possibilities became apparent.

The core CB+P creative team responsible for Subservient Chicken included then–interactive creative director (now co-CCO) Jeff Benjamin, copywriter Bob Cianfrone, art director Mark Taylor, associate creative director Rob Reilly and the agency's creative leader, ECD Alex Bogusky. The extended team included CP+B tech lead Jordan Kilpatrick, the Barbarian Group team of Keith Butters, Rick Webb, Benjamin Palmer and others, and the complete list of contributors included pretty much the entire staff of both agencies, who added to the chicken's repertoire of actions.

CP+B's Benjamin says that the site did mark a turning point in terms of the viral distribution of ad messages, but that its massive impact also came from its technology-enabled, gee-whiz quality.

"It changed the model a bit," says Benjamin.

There was the notion before if you wanted eyeballs on digital work, you had to do banners and a media buy. But this was just a web site. The media distribution happened through people passing it on. That had, of course, happened with other things—things that some dude did in his garage. But I think it was one of the first times it happened with a piece of advertising for a big brand. And there was that notion of magic. When you looked at all the interactive advertising at the time, there was some nicely designed stuff, there was some animated stuff, etc. I don't know how much was super interactive, though. And here you have this thing that behaves in a magical way—I ask it to do something and it does it. There was just that quality that you didn't know that something like this could exist. And it was fun—to play with and to tell your friend about it. There was a social currency—you felt kind of cool telling your buddy about it.

In response to the brief for the Tender Crisp Chicken sandwich, the team of writer Bob Cianfrone and art director Mark Taylor had come up with the idea of a subservient chicken and had envisioned a series of TV spots in which a chicken was doing someone's bidding.

Months earlier, the agency had created a banner for Virgin Atlantic that allowed viewers to test out pickup lines on a female subject, who would seemingly react to the flirtational gambits selected by the user. When the Burger King team presented the initial subservient chicken idea to Bogusky, he pushed the interactive element. "Alex was into the interactive part," says Benjamin. "When we started developing the campaign he said 'what if you did the site where you could ask the chicken to do things and it would do it?' That's where it was all born. When I look back on it, it started as a TV campaign, but like a lot of things here, a lot of times it's the medium that you put the idea in that makes a difference. That was the best place for the idea to live."

And then the people at Crispin and the Barbarian Group had to figure out how to actually execute the idea. "We didn't know exactly how we would make it," says Benjamin. "It was unclear if we could shoot that many things, if we could figure out the artificial intelligence and to make it so it would be accurate. It was one of those projects where I remember being fearful. But we partnered with the Barbarian Group, they worked on the AI part and got it to the point where it would work."

In a detailed breakdown of the Subservient Chicken production process on the Barbarian Group's blog on the occasion of the site's fifth anniversary, Rick Webb, co-founder and COO of the Barbarian Group explains the group's initial take on the tech solution and the initial team involved: "Keith and I rapidly envisioned using a series of video clips tagged with a bunch of keywords that would parse a text input string from a user and show the right clip, thus giving the appearance of a constant video feed. . . . So, then, things kicked into high gear. . . . I assigned Jennifer Iwanicki, our director of production at the time, to handle the project management on our end. I acted as the information architect, and Keith was the Flash developer. Aubrey, our CTO, kept an eye on the tech side and worked on server stuff with Jordan Kilpatrick at Crispin, whose title at the time was 'Web Geek.'"[2]

Crispin's Benjamin says his team made a fake web site for internal use at the agency that featured a Photoshopped picture of agency creative director Dave Schiff in a chicken suit. It was distributed to everyone in the agency to solicit ideas for what people would ask of the fowl in order to build a database of commands. "We got thousands of different commands," says Benjamin. "But when we sorted though them we figured out people kept asking the same stuff over and over. Some sort of weird psychology that when you can ask anything you only ask certain things."

The Crispin and Barbarian teams shot the chicken man performing 400-odd actions over the course of a day in an L.A. apartment. Benjamin says the site was originally intended to have audio but "we were laughing so hard during the shoot we had to take it out."

When the site was nearly ready, the two teams sent the link out to a few people in their respective circles, and hours later the thing had taken off.

The campaign represented a new copywriting challenge. Bob Cianfrone, the copywriter on the project, contributed to the creation of one of the bigger moments in digital marketing to date; in the day-to-day job of getting Subservient Chicken made, he, together with others in the agency, also had to write what was in the heads of millions of unknown poultry dominators. "It's a good example of copywriting in the digital world," says Benjamin. "It's not just about beautiful copy but it's thinking about how people speak, being a master of language."

Subservient Chicken represented the increasingly collaborative creative process and the blurring of lines between creative and production—and between creativity and technology—that are characteristic of digital campaigns. "It was a perfect creative execution using readily understood technologies but in new, interesting creative ways," says Webb. "Everyone was talking about Flash video, but they were all thinking of it like television. The chicken was a great orthogonal approach to what the tech could do: interesting tech as envisioned by knowledgeable creatives. We had been using this as a competitive edge in our process already, but this solidified that approach and ingrained it into our company throughout (and I suspect into CP+B as well)."

As a result of the digital revolution, the creative team has expanded beyond the copywriter/art director paradigm, and not just because it takes a village to come up with commands for a chicken.

Traditionally, a copywriter and art director were given a creative brief—a marketing challenge boiled down by the agency's strategic thinkers—and would put their heads together and come up with a campaign. That is, they would come up with an overarching idea, articulated in one or a series of ads for which media space would be purchased. In fact, in the decades leading up to the digital explosion that coincided roughly with the turn of the century, copywriters and art directors were creating ads for media that had already been purchased by a media company that wasn't in the same building or even part of the same corporation as that creative team's agency. Media and creative, two sides of the same coin, had been surgically separated in the early '90s in the interest of maximum shareholder value for agency holding companies, and so the ad industry entered the digital age already creatively hobbled. As CP+B's Benjamin said of Subservient Chicken, media is part of the idea. This is true for any campaign. But the ad industry had ignored this fact in favor of media buying efficiencies and agency networks' bottom lines.

These chickens, it seemed, came home to roost when the media world exploded and brand creativity started to become a limitless proposition. The best ad ideas were bigger, more integrated, more in tune with how people were consuming and sharing media, and not respectful of platform boundaries. Yet the industry's big agency players were typically structured in silos—media over here, "creative" here, digital over there, PR somewhere else. Agencies like CP+B that grew from scratch with media and creativity bundled together, smaller startup shops and digital agencies started to gain ground as the media world shifted, creating campaigns that were in keeping with the digital age.

When a brand idea involved TV, print and outdoor, a copywriter and an art director generated scripts and lines. Production companies then made films out of scripts. Directors of commercials often added substantially to the scripts, but the line between creation and execution was visible.

That's changed. As digital brand creativity came to the fore, writers remained key players in the process. But now, writers were coming up with ideas that came with a lot of questions, like: "How do we do this?" or "Can we do this?"

NO COPYWRITER IS AN ISLAND

Joel Kaplan, a copywriter with credits on some of the 00s significant digital campaigns, including the much-awarded Halo 3 "Believe" and Burger King "Whopper Sacrifice" campaigns, started as a receptionist at a full-service L.A. agency before moving to AKQA, which was, and is, one of the industry's top digital agencies. Kaplan is one of a generation of creatives who set out to be an ad writer just at the time the industry was shifting toward digital, and his experience demonstrates the evolving notions of copywriting and of the creative team and the blurring of boundaries between creative and production.

"When I got out of school, I had a book that was 90 percent print and some guerrilla stuff. At schools you were still learning traditional stuff—they were just starting to talk about non-traditional work. That was considered guerrilla. I interviewed everywhere and I eventually started doing freelance and was then brought in at AKQA San Francisco." At the time, Kaplan, like many other ad professionals and aspirants, looked upon digital as the industry's ugly stepchild. "And then I started working on Sprite, on the 'Sublymonal' campaign. When I started working on it I quickly realized that I liked coming up with these crazy new ideas. In school, I thought you had to make an ad, something that was a recognizable thing. But I found we were doing something different. Each time you worked on something you had to ask yourself, could this physically be done? That was the first awakening where I realized that advertising was changing. Instead of coming up with a new TV spot or whatever that fit into a space that already worked we came up with things that didn't look like advertising in a medium that we weren't sure would pan out."

It was the early, heady days of web 2.0. "People were starting to talk about a site called YouTube; Facebook wasn't around yet. All we knew was that everyone was asking themselves, if you went to a desert island and you could bring a TV, a magazine or a computer, which would you bring? And everyone said computer. So we started saying well, why aren't we doing more advertising for people interacting with computers?"

At that time, the copywriter/art director team was still in effect. But on its periphery was a growing contingent of new players helping to bring a new kind of idea to life. "We were still paired up," says Kaplan, "but instead of being in your own world where it was just your team, there were a lot of outside members you would talk to. There were interaction designers, flash designers, and motion graphics designers and we'd walk down the hall and ask, 'if we do this, could we do this and this?' And that circle expanded. It wasn't just a team of two; there were more people involved both on the technical and production side. I can write a headline, but when it comes time to build a user interface for a mobile app, I can't do that process on my own."

CP+B's Benjamin says the idea of the creative team has evolved at the agency.

It's been a bit of a voyage. When I came here, we were running out of space in Miami. So, in a small room it was me, a Flash designer, a back end developer, an art director and a chair where the producer who was producing 90 projects at one point sat. All of us were crammed into a room. We weren't always brainstorming with each other but we were always there for each other. I set it up intentionally at first so that there were no writers. I wanted to force collaboration between interactive and traditional people. I thought, if you started hiring art directors and copywriters for interactive, there would be no need for them to interact with other creatives. If there were no writers on this team, they would have to go to traditional teams to work with them.

As the agency grew, teams expanded to include interactive writers, and the agency brought a significant amount of tech capability in house.[3] Teams got a bit more siloed, says Benjamin. "It was like a baton you passed from group to group. The work got a bit worse." At that time the agency was working on Burger King Games—which saw creative teams creating three fully functional video games that the burger chain sold at its restaurants—and Benjamin and his team spent time at a game development company for an up-close view of how they worked. He found that they are structured around slightly larger teams that include writers, visual artists, producers and tech people all sitting together and working together, which is more like the structure CP+B had previously through an accident of space shortage, says Benjamin.

> It was clear we had to get back to that, so our teams became pods that would have a writer, and then maybe a developer and an interaction designer and, depending on the account, a producer. I think that's the future of creative teams, especially for digital work. You have all those people sitting together. They might not be brainstorming all the time, but they're always there for each other; they feel like they are, creatively, a team. When we brought the technology piece in house we made it a point to say, this isn't a production capability, this is a creative capability. A technologist is as creative, in a way, as a writer. The reality is that teams change depending on what the project is and who the people are. You might have one team that is super nerdy and they might not need a developer; you might put a producer with them. But the end result is that the team is now much bigger than art director/copywriter. You're not going to get very far in this day and age with just that team.

The expanded creative team is interpreted differently at agencies of different size and type (and is discussed further in chapter 7).

But, in general, the creative team that is composed exclusively of an art director and a writer is, more and more, a rarity. Again, this is not a signal of the declining relevance of the writer. It means that the scope of the writer's work and the potential of the writer's ideas have expanded. There are also an ever-expanding range of scenarios and companies for writers to work in.

There are a range of digital companies that use copywriters in different ways. The Barbarian Group, the company that helped bring Subservient Chicken to life, began as what could most accurately be described as a digital production company. A wiry start-up stocked with entrepreneurial nerds, the company typically partnered with full-service agencies to enhance digital ideas and provide the technical know-how to get them made. As it grew, TBG started to become a new kind of agency, working directly with brands, creating interactive ideas in tandem with agencies and other creative partners, and developing its own software and digital product.

In addition to building things like Subservient Chicken and Methods ComeClean.com, a site where visitors could partake of a sort of digital confession, unloading their transgressions and then washing them away, the shop has created sites for marketers like VW and Comcast. It partnered with CNN on a web-meets-real-world effort that placed a t-shirt icon next to select headlines on CNN.com and allowed visitors to order a shirt emblazoned with their favorite headline.

For marketing behemoth GE, the shop created a simple blog through which TBG staffers discussed the serious science that GE was dropping in its various business sectors like health and transport. Later, the blog turned into a web series, *The GE Show.* "The traditional craft of copywriting and branding and positioning the brand and finding the exact right thing to say, those things that copywriters have always done," says Webb, "that is totally different than writing the GE blog." Webb says TBG commonly uses writers from the journalism world for generating web site copy and content.

The shop created a site for organic food company Kashi that Webb describes as a platform through which campaigns are run. "When we launched it there was zero traditional copywriting—it was just things like naming navigation elements. Now, campaigns come out of the site—there might be a module where you can sign up to get a free cookie, or content-based stuff we would hire an editor to do or a campaign around a certain product that will have, say, a game one month or a video. Each of those will use copy in different ways."

Since Subservient Chicken, many digitally focused campaigns have made magic, upping the ante on what's possible in the real and virtual worlds, and what's possible for writers. There has been an unmistakable shift in budgets and creative energy toward the digital space. Meanwhile, as noted, as awards season rolls around, the most coveted honors, more coveted perhaps than the film category awards, have come to be for the digital and "emerging media"-type awards, like the Cannes Titanium Lions.

Kaplan contributed to one of the biggest award winners of the 2008 season, the integrated Halo 3 "Believe" effort out of McCann Erickson's T.A.G. unit and AKQA in San Francisco. The campaign centered on a 2,100-square-foot diorama built by Stan Winston Studios that depicted a battle from the game. The core of the campaign in this case was an epic TV spot from T.A.G. writer Rick Herrera and art director Ben Wolan and directed by Rupert Sanders that took viewers on a journey through the battle, captured in an intricately detailed monument. The AKQA team translated the diorama to a web experience. "We ended up saying look, you have this huge model," says Kaplan. "Instead of shooting it for the spot and throwing it away, we wanted to bring the battle to life. We wanted to let people explore every nuance of it, to add another layer to the Believe story." The campaign was lauded as the year's top integrated campaign, winning the Grand Prix in the Integrated category at Cannes (the spot also won a Grand Prix in the film category) and the top prize at the Andy Awards, the Grandy.

CP+B kept pace with another handful of landmark digitally leaning efforts. In 2009, Jeff Benjamin's team, working under ECDs Rob Reilly and Andrew Keller, created Whopper Sacrifice, a Facebook app that allows users of the social network to ice their marginal friends in favor of a coupon for the famous burger. Kaplan, the writer on the project, says the idea came out of a back-and-forth session with Benjamin, art director Neil Hayman and associate tech director Matt Renauro.

> We sat in the office one day throwing ideas around, talking about Facebook. Now we think of Facebook as having been around for so long, but at the time (the end of 2008), most people had only been on it about 6 months. It was when everyone you knew was finally on it and you were becoming friends with all these people and we were talking about the frustrations of that—what does it even mean that I'm friends with someone online. We were laughing about it—these people you haven't known in forever—what's the value of them? And we started talking about, "What's better,

an online friend or blank?" And Jeff looks over and says maybe we do it so we start putting Whoppers against things. Maybe you can see what's better—a friend or a whopper—let's see what people go for. So we played with that and came up with the idea we called Whopper Sacrifice.

The campaign proved short-lived (Facebook shut the fun down soon after it started) but successful, with 200,000 friends sacrificed in a little over a week. Naturally, the campaign was covered by media outlets of all sizes and stripes, generating 35 million media impressions, according to CP+B's estimates.

THE POST-DIGITAL AGE

Increasingly, the expertise and the sensibilities that came out of the digital revolution are being applied to brand initiatives that transcend the internet, or any other medium. Some of the most compelling campaigns of recent days have had web components and have harnessed what you might call the digital ethic in their use of technology, social media, collaborative creative process, interactive elements, but have been rooted in real-world experience.

Two examples: the VW "Fun Theory" campaign out of DDB Stockholm and Pepsi's "Refresh Everything" initiative out of TBWA\Chiat\Day L.A.

The Fun Theory was based on a number of experiments to test whether people would be more inclined to behave responsibly if it were fun to do so. Creatives made a set of giant piano keys out of a stairway in a Stockholm subway (a la *Big*); they installed a device in garbage bins that made a cartoonish, dropping-off-a-cliff sound when people deposited trash. The experiments led back to a site that tied in VW's environmentally responsible cars, and encouraged people to submit their own fun theory idea.

"In a way what I think is happening is that online behavior is affecting most other areas of life at the moment," says Andreas Dahlqvist, ECD of DDB Stockholm, the agency behind Fun Theory. "We see interactivity and social components everywhere now. There is huge potential in using digital to enhance 'real life' experience, and I think we are just seeing the beginning of that. It's adding a new layer of value, a fourth dimension if you like. Looking at it the other way around, it's about making digital tangible. I think there is a need to add 'realness' in an increasingly digitized world."

Pepsi made news in 2010 when it announced that instead of placing ads in the Super Bowl, as it had famously done for decades, it would use that mega media budget to fund a crowdsourced project for social good. Pepsi and Chiat\Day invited individuals and organizations to submit practical "shovel-ready" ideas for social and environmental good to refresheverything.com (more on the campaign in chapter 8).

The line between digital campaigns and just plain brand creativity is fading. Indeed, the line between digital agencies and traditional or full-service agencies is fading too. Digital agencies have distinguished themselves for bringing together the technical expertise and aptitude for creating relevant, useful things that reflect the way people actually behave; traditional agencies have historically been the lead dogs at brand strategy, storytelling. Those worlds are moving toward each other at a breakneck pace. One can safely predict a time soon when the "digital" prefix will disappear from most agencies.

The new generation agencies that started up toward the end of the 00s have already dispensed with the distinction. Pereira & O'Dell (which hired Kaplan in 2009) was cofounded by one of the digital world's biggest creative names, PJ Pereira, who had won multiple awards as a digital creative in Brazil and then had gone on to more success at digital shop AKQA. Based on the creative product coming out of his agency, it's impossible to accurately apply a label to it. The shop employs a range of creative talents, including ECD Kash Sree, a creative most known for his award-winning commercials for Nike while he worked at Wieden + Kennedy. Pereira & O'Dell's latest efforts have included a huge campaign for Lego encompassing a web film, a community site and a mobile app; a web video for Muscle Milk called *Sexy Pilgrim*, which became a viral hit and a series of print ads for the University of Phoenix.

"What I'm trying to do here is to train and prepare our teams internally to stop thinking about digital as a separate thing," says Pereira. "We need to think about people, and how they live. Of course digital is a huge part of that; it's the one thing that can't be left behind. But I don't want my teams here to be so obsessed with digital that they start to do gimmickry. I don't want them to do things because they're new but instead because they are meaningful and interesting."

So what are the copywriting lessons from the digital age? It seems that the digital copywriter, or rather the copywriter of the post-digital age, has an almost impossibly broad mandate—she must be an ideator, writer, tech expert, collaborator, sociologist, social media guru. And, well, yes, if you are talking about the agency copywriter's job, it has inarguably become more complex. But, if you break it down, the job of the copywriter still revolves around some fundamental things.

As a post-digital copywriter you are:

A CREATOR OF IDEAS

Kaplan, who has also taught advertising at the Miami Ad School, says agencies are looking for the golden combination of writer and big-picture thinker. "I would tell my students, there are only so many roles at an agency—agencies aren't getting any bigger, typically. If I see an amazing writer, that's great. But if see an amazing writer that can't come up with solutions for a client I can't use you."

It's also about making ideas happen, having an eye for execution, says Kaplan. "Your job as a creative isn't just to come up with ideas that are interesting; it's also the follow-through. It's coming up with an idea and taking it the step to make it come to life in the right way. I tend to do that best through words. A technical director does it best through user experience. Together we're a great team."

A MASTER OF THE CRAFT

The writer who thinks in ideas, has an awareness of tech, and is an inspired storyteller writes her own ticket. Even in the digital world, writers write. Perhaps the first thing to establish if you're interested in digital ideas, in big ideas of any description, is are you also interested in writing?

As we've established, all creative roles are blurring together, especially in the digital space. Writers are working with an expanding team of creative, technical and production talents, on projects that may look nothing like an ad. But remember, the writer is still responsible for writing.

There are other roles in the creative process—user-experience designer, interaction designer, strategist, tech lead, producer. You might well be a bit of all of those things, and many creatives today strive to be so-called T-shaped people—those with a core strength but capabilities across a range of disciplines. But if you aim to be a copywriter, writing must be a passion. It must interest you and you must work on it.

A CONVERSATIONALIST

Many of the creatives interviewed for this book had a common comment: the craft of writing is diminishing, and it's hard to find people who can crank out the big ideas, but can also write. Many others pooh-poohed the lamentations for the lost art of writing as just another kind of "better back in the day" nostalgia.

But one thing that is true is that there are more different kinds of writing in demand now, kinds that didn't really exist in advertising's past, so it's hard to know if our notions of craft are too tied to legacy ad formats.

The best writers of the past crafted brilliant headlines and memorable body copy in which each sentence was burnished to perfection, each word chosen to convey a product attribute or set a brand tone.

Now there are, to put it simply, more kinds of things to write. And the digital age has meant that more of those things are interactive in nature—the rise of social media has meant that marketing has evolved into an ongoing conversation with an engaged consumer. Writers must be experts in sustaining that conversation. "I think that creatives and marketers using social media have to realize that the medium allows for two way conversations," says Chris Brogan, president of New Marketing Labs and author of *Social Media 101*. "The most beautiful thing about social media is that you can actually talk instead of pitch and copywrite. The organizations who use this best . . . will benefit the most."

Nicke Bergstrom, co-founder of famed Swedish digital agency FarFar, now a creative director at Mother New York, likens creating campaigns to going on a date. "If you were sitting across from someone and all you were doing was talking and not allowing the other person to say anything, it wouldn't be very successful."

Does that ability to hold a conversation represent the same basic writing ability inherent in writing a paragraph of ad copy? There are writers who can do both, and more. But, as we'll discuss in chapter 6, many agencies are looking to different talent pools—like comedy, journalism and longer-form entertainment—for writers with a conversational sensibility.

Guy Barnett, a former Ogilvy creative director and co-founder of New York agency The Brooklyn Brothers, says,

> Most people would argue the great age of copywriting is over. And it's true that few can hand-carve a phrase like the Davids Abbott and Ogilvy, or Tim Delaney. Or even Neil French. They wrote like Clarence Darrow spoke—like lawyers persuading a jury.
>
> They articulated and romanced the minutiae of a product to showcase its most desirable qualities. So, by the time you reached the clever—quick-nod-to-the-headline—last line of their eloquent prose, you had been reasoned into buying whatever they were selling. Case closed.
>
> That was an age when advertising was all about persuasion. Now it's all about engagement. And that's a lot harder—which is why we bemoan a dearth of skill.

Barnett says a writer now must have an even stronger "power over language." Says Barnett:

> Your choice of phrasing and syntax needs to be that much more nimble and unusual. You need to keep people both entertained and informed. You need to be authoritative, charming, funny. You need to be able to recount a story and digress in all directions. You need to be able to do it in a variety of voices so you can work on a number of brands. And you need to be able to express yourself in 140 characters or less as well as at length on the back of the packaging. And there simply aren't that many writers who can do that. Actually, there are; they just don't see advertising as a career. We call them authors. Or columnists. Or journalists. Or bloggers. The role of the writer in advertising is more vital than ever because, despite what many people think, people read more than ever. They read blogs, magazines, Harry Potter, and Facebook updates. They read all the time. Gossage said that "people read what interests them, sometimes that's an ad." He's still right. Except sometimes it's a tweet.

A DEALER IN EMOTIONS

For all the ways ad creatives differ in how they describe the job—whether it's brand storytelling, brand utility or plain old advertising—

most of them will agree on one thing: among their prime directives is building an emotional connection with an audience.

Emotions aren't just the stuff of classic narratives, of commercials. The best digital experiences play to emotions.

Jeff Benjamin started his career at an early digital agency, Modem Media, and moved to San Francisco's Goodby Silverstein & Partners, known then as a full-service shop strong on narrative and craft (the agency has since become a case study in a traditional agency effectively incorporating the digital mindset). "I went there because I wanted to make people laugh; I wanted to tell stories through digital. At that time I wasn't getting the opportunity to do that where I was. For the most part I was doing direct advertising. At Goodby, I learned how you build brands, how you make people feel something, which is, ironically, maybe the most primal of interactive things. When we say interactive, you think, oh, I got someone to do something, but the more basic part of interactive is to make people feel something."

While acknowledging the power of digital to advance ideas, Pereira emphasizes the emotional imperative to his creatives. He points to an example from earlier in his career—an early banner for the São Paulo Eye Bank that he created through his previous shop, Agencia Click. When viewers moused over Braille copy on the banner, the cursor, now a hand, spelled out the words "Donate Corneas," with the copy fading away when the cursor moved forward. "It was just a banner ad; it's supposed to be boring. But it was touching, because the copy faded back. It was a combination of technology, perception and a feeling you can get from human nature. It was probably one of the first banners that used interactivity to create an emotional response."

AN ANALOG HUMAN BEING

If you're reading this as someone who's starting out in advertising, you probably don't need to be told to immerse yourself in digital experiences, in social media and technology.

But it does bear reminding that even as a digital creative, technology and the online world should not be the extent of your inspiration. As we've seen, ad creatives are no longer necessarily charged with making "ads." They are responsible for creating real content that's relevant to real people's lives. The best new ad experiences are those that harness the power of digital and apply it to the real world.

Advertising types say their job is to mine human truths, an expression that's become a horrible cliché in the industry. But the best work does just that. Whopper Sacrifice took a novel human problem that was arising from the use of Facebook—the perplexing notion and questionable value of virtual "friends"—and turned it into a wickedly fun and funny brand experience.

In creating the web experience for the Halo 3 "Believe" campaign, Kaplan says he turned to a decidedly analog storytelling source—the documentaries of Ken Burns—for inspiration on how his team would present the battle narrative to web viewers.

Understanding technology is important, but Pereira says the best ideas and the best work come from a combination of insights from different places. "It could be an insight into an athlete's mind, a technique an artist created, a glimpse of brilliance you get from a classic book and a new technology that Apple just launched. It's a flash that comes from watching a fashion show and watching your grandma talking to your son. The greatest ideas always come not from a single source but from a combination of sources. That's when it gets original. That's when you as a creative can bring a new perspective to something that cannot be replicated randomly just because someone is watching the same thing you are. Technology is powerful because it brings a sense of freshness and cool factor but if you rely just on that it's shallow; that's when it becomes a gimmick."

A UTILITARIAN

Some of the best brand ideas of the past decade have been utilities, things that make people's lives easier or better, in large or small ways. Nike+, Fiat eco:Drive. These aren't narratives in the usual sense, but they convey a brand's story.

As Nick Law, EVP/chief creative officer, R/GA North America, says, some people think in stories, some people think in systems. Both are part of the overall brand experience. User interface is an increasingly important part of the brand equation. This is not to say copywriters need to be wunderkind programmers or UX designers, but it does mean that copywriters can expect to be working with people who are those things and it does mean that all creatives should be asking: "Is what I'm creating adding something to someone's life? Is it useful, entertaining or beautiful?"

"For the past few decades, ad agencies have been coming up with long-term strategic platforms on which creative expressions can be based," says Rei Inamoto, global creative director at AKQA. "That 'platform' mostly has been messaging platforms—a declaration of the brand rather than any action to participate in. If communication is about 'saying,' products/services are about 'doing.' Ad agencies have mostly been about saying. In order to stay relevant in the next decade and beyond, agencies need to be also about 'doing.'"

AN EXPLAINER, A CLARIFIER

One of the skills from the digital space that serves any copywriter well is the ability to make the complicated simple.

"If you look at what came out of the early days of digital, when everything was about banners, one of the things that carries over to this day, and the challenge of a lot of writers, when you're writing for sites and apps and anything else, is simplicity," says Benjamin. "There is a tendency to want to be super creative, and of course you should be creative as a writer. But in many cases, copy has the added burden of being beautiful or making you laugh, but also clearly telling you what to do. The notion of instructional copy to make an ad work can be a challenge for writers."

Whopper Sacrifice was a great example. "The writing for that was especially important," says Benjamin. "At the end of the day it was a utility. We looked at that copy over and over again. People think, oh just make a thing where you delete a friend—but it had to be funny, it couldn't be mean, and it had to be clear what you had to do because Facebook apps were complicated to some people. Those were big challenges for a writer to take on."

STUDY THE COMPANIES THAT DON'T ADVERTISE

For most of the last several decades, aspiring copywriters and creatives studied the annals of advertising for inspiration—award show annuals, issues of *Creativity* and *Communication Arts*. But today's creatives should expand their perspective. Study the ways of the companies that were born and became brand powers in the internet age, like Amazon and Google, and, on a smaller scale, Etsy.

Zappos is a great example in that it's a company whose meteoric rise was based in large part on its devotion to customer service, a devotion that Zappos watchers describe as fanatical, bordering on weird. "We put as much energy in planning and training our employees as other companies do planning their media," Brian Kalma, director of creative services/brand management told *Creativity* in 2008. "That allows us to feel more comfortable having every single employee be a direct contact with the customer. Every person is an advertising vehicle; with thousands of phone calls a day, multiplied by 365, those are a huge amount of touch points with our customers."

Study what your favorite companies do from a complete user-experience perspective, from product to the way their web sites work, through service.

You might not be able to architect a customer service infrastructure, but you'll start orienting your work toward what speaks to people and away from just broadcasting ad slogans.

CHAPTER 5

HOW TO NOT WRITE
ADVERTISING

So, if we've got this right, copywriters today are storytellers, conversation keepers, curators and inventors. They are idea generators, executors and technology savants.

On any given day, depending on where and for whom they work, these new masters and mistresses of brand creativity and engagement might be writing a script for a web film, orchestrating a transmedia story or conceiving and helping to develop an app. They might be inventing a way for an automaker to contribute to the conversation on conservation by creating an application to encourage efficient driving; they might be working with a handful of top young artists to create a giant Times Square billboard for a retailer and then repurposing that billboard into limited-edition handbags designed by Ana Sui, as Mother New York recently did for Target; or they might be coming up with commands to give to a chicken. It's a veritable creative wonderland out there.

But an explosion of creative opportunities doesn't mean copywriters can escape the scourge that has faced writers from the dawn of written expression: the blank page.

That page may no longer be made of wood pulp. And the warm-up ritual may not be the sharpening of a carbon-based writing implement (though, as we'll discuss in the following pages, no matter what the assignment, some copywriters say that either writing or sketching things out with a pencil is an essential step on the road to an idea). But with each new project, today's copywriter shoulders the same burden of expectation that has bent every ad creative for the past 150 years and stares into the same yawning void that no three midday martinis could ever fill.

So you're some kind of copywriter, faced with some kind of assignment. What do you do? Where do you start?

FIRST OF ALL, FORGET ABOUT MAKING AN AD

In the seminal copywriting book *Hey Whipple, Squeeze This,* first published in 1998, Luke Sullivan noted: "When you sit down to do an ad, you're competing with every brand out there."

That was and remains partially true in the sense that you certainly aren't just competing with Brand A's main rival, Brand Z. You are competing with every other brand vying for a share of a consumer's money and attention.

But as we've discussed on previous pages, today, as a copywriter or other brand creativity maestro, you're not just making something that will compete with other brands and with other messages created by brands. You're making something to compete with every other piece of content, every other media experience that a person has during her waking hours. So you are charged with making something that stands on its own as a worthwhile thing for a person to engage with, brand or no brand. It's just that, at the same time, you also have to make the content or experience work for the company or brand involved. "We moved our goalposts," says Dave Bedwood, creative director and co-founder of U.K. digital agency Lean Mean Fighting Machine. "There is no point making advertising that is better than other advertising; that is not your competitor for people's time. You are up against all of the things they want to watch and read, the content they are seeking out. We are under no illusion that we can suddenly make popular content that is as good as *24* or *Lost* or write long copy that is as good as Malcolm Gladwell's latest book, but if that is the goal, then your work has a much better chance of making an impact with your audience."

Yes, there are more ad messages to compete with. We're talking about brand ubiquity—more messages, more logos, more general brand presence over more channels. At some point over the last several years, you've likely seen some sort of quantification of the noise level in the ad environment; in a 1998 magazine article, marketing guru Seth Godin tossed out the number 3,000—the average American is exposed to 3,000 ad messages a day.[1] That number has been regurgitated in countless articles and news segments spanning about ten years. More recently, the number 5,000 has been thrown around.

Is it 3,000? 5,000? Or more like 300 or 50,000? And what counts as an ad message? An actual ad? A logo? Strolling by product labels in the supermarket? Well, it sort of doesn't matter because those numbers are at best only a part of the story and at worst a red herring when you're thinking about the challenges of making something relevant for a brand and a consumer. The above numbers are insufficient to describe the shift in behavior that has accompanied the rise of the internet and the widespread adoption of broadband.

This increase in brand presence has coincided with a decrease in available uninterrupted attention as the internet ushered in the age of multitasking. And yet more significant, the explosion of branding has coincided with the age of the empowered media consumer, the media consumer who is also now a media producer.

If you're under 35, if you're watching TV at all, you're often also doing at least one other thing (texting, talking, "co-viewing," i.e., commenting on the show you're watching via Twitter or other social service, posting a hilarious picture of Mr. Mittens on LOLCats) with at least one other screen. Much has been made of the effects of internet-enabled distraction on human cognition and culture. In his book *The Shallows,* Nicholas Carr warns of the brain-softening effects of the internet—as people grow accustomed to consuming smaller bits of information, each interrupted by the next, we lose the kind of deep thinking and "deep reading" that was associated with offline reading, aka reading books.

Carr says: "We want to be interrupted, because each interruption brings us a valuable piece of information. . . . And so we ask the Internet to keep interrupting us, in ever more and different ways. We willingly accept the loss of concentration and focus, the division of our attention and the fragmentation of our thoughts, in return for the wealth of compelling or at least diverting information we receive. Tuning out is not an option many of us would consider."[2]

In a *New York Magazine* piece called "In Defense of Distraction," Sam Anderson writes: "The tech theorist Linda Stone famously coined the phrase 'continuous partial attention' to describe our newly frazzled state of mind. American office workers don't stick with any single task for more than a few minutes at a time; if left uninterrupted, they will most likely interrupt themselves. Since every interruption costs around 25 minutes of productivity, we spend nearly a third of our day recovering from them. We keep an average of eight windows open on our computer screens at one time and skip between them every twenty seconds. . . . People who frequently check their e-mail have tested as less intelligent than people who are actually high on marijuana."[3]

For every writer and theorist who proclaims that the "internet is making us dumb," there are others, like Anderson, who say digital culture is, arguably, shaping better brains and encouraging what could be viewed as more positive societal behavior. In the 2010 book *Cognitive Surplus: Creativity and Generosity in a Connected Age,* Clay Shirky notes the astounding figures on TV consumption: Americans consume 200 billion hours of TV a year; someone born in 1960 has already watched 50,000 hours of TV. Shirky talks about the vast potential the damned distracting internet has created—as people shift from being passive consumers of media (from watching TV, and ads) to being creators and participants (contributing to Wikipedia, making and posting videos to YouTube, creating Facebook groups and blogs).[4]

There's a lot more to say and much that can be debated about kids today and why Jayden can't read the Cliffs Notes on *Moby Dick,* never mind the novel. The point here is to determine what this fact of consumer culture means for a copywriter whose job is to earn someone's attention and translate that attention into action. The starting point is not to figure out how to make a formulaic thing called an ad that stands out among 5,000 other ads. It's how to connect with a person who is dealing with you on his own terms. How do you make that person want to interact with your creation, want to share your offering with others. How do you matter to him?

In an industry that has an embarrassing predilection for catchphrases and clichés, "marketing is a conversation" has joined the ranks of groanworthy adspeak. But there's no getting around it. Consumers have voices, they have the means to have a conversation with whomever they want about a brand, whether the brand is part of that conversation or not.

So, copywriters have a gargantuan challenge to be relevant, but also a great opportunity to be original, to interact with an audience, to have people talk about, spread and engage with the things they create.

"There's been a real cultural shift," says R/GA's Nick Law, "away from people believing or even caring what you're telling them in an ad anymore. What matters is if a brand fits into my life somehow."

Nancy Vonk, co-chief creative officer of Ogilvy Toronto, says her message to her agency's creatives is

> to think of themselves as problem solvers, not ad makers. Ideally, begin every assignment looking directly at the business problem (or opportunity) and push up against that with media-neutral thinking. If a client has asked for a print ad or banner ad or what- ever specific medium, ignore that and look for a big idea. A great idea that truly solves the problem will be able to channel into that print ad, etc. The client will see the specific medium they requested, but in the context of a holistic solution that can potentially inform many spaces.
>
> You use a very different lens if you're hunting for a TV spot ("ok, so I have just 30 seconds to tell a story, here's the kind of short story I can tell") versus looking for a solution that could be literally anything. I tell people they aren't allowed to show me TV scripts in the first round of ideas, if that's what the client asked for. Recently a team [proposed] a bake shop when a print ad was asked for. The print ad happened, but it was one small component of a totally un- expected, refreshing solution.

For the sake of simplicity, we've employed the term "advertising" in these pages, but perhaps one of the essential messages to take away from this book is that your job isn't to create "an ad." It's to create something useful, entertaining or beautiful (or all of the above) on behalf of a brand.

IT'S NOT ABOUT THE "JUICINESS OF THE MEAT." IT'S ABOUT HUMAN BEINGS.

Not every campaign that you, the modern copywriter, work on will be an inspired example of a compelling conversation; not every assignment will afford you the opportunity to reinvent a brand and conceive a category-changing idea that will net you a Cannes Grand Prix and land you in a different tax bracket. You will be writing print ads and TV commercials, web site copy and flyers, full stop. But the same qualities—entertainment, utility, beauty—can still be built into the most quotidian ad assignment. If you are distributing your message on a paid media channel (on a TV show or as an ad in a print magazine, let's say), assume that you have the most vanishingly tiny chance of a person's pausing to hear you out (you do). Assume that they don't give a rat's ass about the science concerning brand X's new formulation you're about to drop on them (they don't). Assume the person is like you and wants something that's going to make her laugh, help her life, make a great story to pass on, make her think, make her feel.

And that's the basic challenge. Technology and technique are important, as we've seen from some of the breakthrough campaigns of the last several years, but at its root, your challenge is to make a connection with a human being.

Johannes Leonardo founder Leo Premutico says, "The first and foremost thing we are looking for in people is that inherent passion to touch people with their ideas. John Lennon said it best when he was once asked why he wrote music. He responded by comparing it to writing a letter. Writing the letter, he said, got him excited but what he really got off on was the response he would get to that letter. That's it at its essence. We're looking for people who have that thing inside them, that urge to touch people with their ideas, those who live for simplifying things down to a common language that affects people, deeply and broadly."

Says CP+B's Bill Wright: "It's one of the things that hasn't changed—finding that magic moment when you've come up with the insight that will make people think, I've thought of that a hundred times but I never thought of saying it like that. It's that moment of connection where people think there's a kindred spirit out there."

Creating ideas that affect people is probably best undertaken under the assumption that those people, to paraphrase Ogilvy, are not morons. "You have to start with the belief that people are intelligent," says Tim Delaney, famed copywriter and founder of agency Leagas Delaney. "A lot of them are more intelligent than I am and more intelligent than people in advertising." Delaney says he still writes, every day. "I like it because it's challenging. There is the top layer of this business that you can say is all charlatans flogging dog food to neurotic pet owners, or worse still, in America, pharma ads from morning till night telling you you're going to die. But on another level the whole business is quite intriguing. You're trying to match people's beliefs with brands and trying to create long-term equity. That's all quite tricky and interesting. It's not a thin industry. It's often depicted as one, but there are a lot of intriguing problems if you want to treat them as such."

According to many creatives, advertising, and the ad process, has to start with the consumer, not with the list of benefits the brand wants to convey.

"When I started in advertising, I was taught to ask if my ideas were big," PJ Pereira wrote in *Creativity*.

> Today, I'd rather ask if they are interesting enough to be worth experiencing on-demand—not only as on-demand TV, but any form of user-initiated media consumption (web, video games, mobile . . .). As the world consumes almost 70 percent of its information in a digital format, controlled by consumers and passed along, marketers are no longer fighting for more attention for the time they bought. We are all trying for a chance to be played, and that's a totally different game. . . . In order to steal any second of someone's time when they have so much to do, see and play with, marketers and their agencies are now forced to create experiences absolutely worth the consumer's time. The good news is that contrary to what some people tried to make us believe, consumers don't mind being advertised to, as long as these ads are interesting enough for them. Otherwise, Nike's "Write the Future" wouldn't have reached 7 million views on YouTube in less than five days.

Pereira says that agencies and creatives are reorienting themselves to offer this demand-worthy content, but that "there is still one piece missing: bringing advertisers to the discussion to reshape the essence of what an assignment really is." For the last 20 or 30 years, agencies have been told by their clients to think in a very specific way, he says, and that was to

> find the core attributes we need to talk about, then the best story to carry them to every consumer we could reach. Some marketers even got to a point where they established best-practices determining how many times a logo should be seen, how many smiles should be displayed in between . . . In an interruption-based model, that may have worked just fine. But think on-demand, and

it doesn't make sense anymore. It's still way too early to try to establish a recipe to make it work—consumers themselves haven't determined their own patterns yet. But we do know one thing: on-demand campaigns work better when you reverse the order we currently use: first, we find an idea that is interesting for the consumer where a brand can play some role, then we find the best way to include the product there somehow.

Bobby Hershfield, one of the writers behind the SEGA Beta 7 campaign, and now an ECD at Mother New York, says, "I try to not to think of what I'm doing as an ad. I think of it as writing. I try and have a point of view. I don't think of it as an ad until I'm done writing what I need to write; then I go back and say how to make it relevant and smart for the brand's message, thinking beyond the brief, beyond the page, to write something that makes me excited and that stretches me, as opposed to sticking to what's been said before."

So your job as a copywriter is to create something so compelling that it will, first, warrant attention and stand out such as to be heard over the sometimes jarring, sometimes numbing noise of our media-oversaturated culture. But that's only part of the task. Your work, once it attracts attention, has to deliver something relevant to the consumer's life.

Oh, and it has to sell something. Sound hard? It is. That's why it's called a job. This book is full of examples of creative work that satisfied all the criteria of ad greatness, work that broke through, that was relevant to consumers on their own terms and that satisfied a marketer's goals. Whopper Sacrifice is one of the better more recent examples.

Joel Kaplan, a writer and creative director who was a copywriter on Whopper Sacrifice and now works with Pereira at his agency Pereira O'Dell, translates the consumer-first philosophy to his creative process. "I try to figure out what's going on with the product or company," says Kaplan.

What are people misunderstanding about it, or what does it want to be? Then I look at what's going on with the world at large. Before, you'd take a look at a product and you'd create a story about it and buy space and put the story out there. You told someone about your product and hoped they were listening. Now we start the other way. You look around at what's going on in the real world, what conversations are happening, what trends are going on, what people are talking about and where they're talking about it. And try to find a way that our product or company can have a voice in that conversation. Look at Whopper Sacrifice. It wasn't about the juiciness of Burger King meat. The original insight was that 5.5 people out of ten prefer a Whopper. So, we know people like the Whopper, how do we prove it? We knew that Facebook was taking off and people were saying yes to all these friends and then not knowing what to do with them. So, it was an observation about what people were doing and then finding a way to have a voice in that conversation. The upside of that is that people don't feel like you're showing them an ad. They feel like they're having a conversation. And if they like that conversation, they like that brand.

WILL IT SPREAD?

An obvious way to assess your brand campaign's appeal to actual human beings is the degree to which it's viewed and shared by those beings.

Even today, it bears noting, the word viral is misused. Press releases trumpeting a new campaign from a national advertiser will still describe one of its components as a "viral video." As we know, you don't create a viral anything. You create a web video, or other content or experience and it gets passed around and picked up and generally goes on to be embraced and spread around or it doesn't.

But what are the qualities of work that has achieved what we used to call virality?

There are some criteria that separate a good idea from a "viral" idea, says Ed Robinson, co-founder of The Viral Factory, the agency responsible for some of the earliest and most viral viral films. The shop's humungous hits have included "Trojan Games," a series of videos for the condom maker featuring some decidedly non-IOC-approved sporting events, "Extreme Sheep LED Art" for Samsung and a hilarious and not really safe for work Diesel video, "SFW XXX," one of the most viewed videos ever on Creativity Online.

"A good idea in a marketing sense is one which symbolizes and expresses the client's proposition in a clear and compelling way," says Robinson. "It is often a single flashbulb image which aligns a product with something eye catching and resonant. Marketing by association or metaphor. It's worked for half a century! With viral there

What you have to do is get the client and everyone else out of

your head. If you write for them no one is going to be happy;

you'll have a good meeting but no one will be happy when the

work is done. You get everyone out of your head. I always say

that in a way doing advertising is the art of self delusion. You

do something and pretend they're going to buy it. Don't limit

yourself by saying, oh, they'll never do it. You have to write

what comes to your head and if it's a good idea, someone will see

something in it.

Greg Hahn, ECD of BBDO New York

are other questions which need to be asked before a good idea can be a viral idea."

The first, says Robinson, is would anyone with no interest in this product care about the idea? "This is key for us—does the idea hold a human truth which goes beyond us (an advertising agency getting paid to flog some stuff) and the client (who thinks only of their product). If it doesn't then it has no viral potential."

There's also the newness factor. "Lots of good marketing ideas are combinations of old ideas, or a refined version of an old marketing staple," says Robinson. "'Good' often means polished and proven. The internet craves newness, an idea which genuinely intrigues and excites its appetite for stimulation. Ideas, as far as the internet is concerned, have nothing to do with advertising. . . . But they have everything to do with re-assessing their world in some meaningful or fanciful way. An idea must have a hook which makes you want to explore it and discuss it with friends—even if that discussion is filled with sniggers and lasts only two minutes. Not many advertising ideas really do that."

Finally, says Robinson, "a viral idea must help express something on behalf of the audience in a way that they can't. Brands employ agencies to help them express their product story; if the idea is to be viral it should help the audience express something to their own audience (their friends and family). This is the hardest facet of viral to articulate. . . . But if we make a work which one person can send to another and it helps them articulate love, loss, fear, hope, etc. then we have something which has viral potential. Much like a hit song, a viral must be 'ownable' by its audience in a way which most art can't."

INSIGHTS, BRIEFS AND BRIEF INSIGHTS

Many of the creatives quoted here talk about insights. A real brand insight is the starting place for anything good that will come out of your creative process. But what's an insight? Where does it come from?

An insight is a new way of thinking about some aspect of a brand and its interface with its consumers. It can arise from a new bit of data about consumers and how they're behaving, it can come from a new behavior, or it can come from a new perspective on some aspect of the brand's life, from distribution to packaging to placement on the shelves. Insights frequently come from account planners and strategists, but just like great ad ideas, they can come from anyone involved in the creative process.

In a blog post for U.K. marketing trade site *Brand Republic*, veteran U.K. creative and founder of agency Chick Smith Trott, Dave Trott said: "An insight is something that you didn't know before. Something that may change the way you think about the problem. An insight can be the first step on the way to an idea. But it isn't an idea. An idea is what you do with the insight. How you turn analysis into synthesis. How that discovery becomes action. Of course, there can be an insight without a subsequent idea. But there can't really be an idea, not a great one, without first having an insight."[5]

"You need some truly surprising or unique insight," says Pelle Sjoenell, one half of the sibling team of Calle and Pelle Sjoenell who are co-ECDs at BBH and responsible for the much awarded Oasis *Dig Out Your Soul* campaign, among other things. "Whether that comes in the brief or it comes from the creatives after they've had the overall brief. Once you latch onto something that's true and interesting, then I think that's the starting point for the creative process."

In the agency context, every brand-creativity initiative starts with a brief. For many creatives, a sharp brief is the most important foundation for an idea, and for most creatives, when it comes to briefs, less is more. Having a clear picture of the problem means ideas can be focused.

"I love the brief that states a problem and nothing else," says Alessandra Lariu, EVP/group CD at McCann Erickson New York. "When you state a problem you can get really juicy solutions, you can come at it from a different perspective and a different angle rather than knowing, OK, here's our target audience, here are the places we need to be, here are solutions."

Lariu and her then-partner Matt O'Rourke spearheaded the creation of the Priceless Picks iPhone app for client MasterCard, based on the simplest possible brief—the company wanted to encourage card holders to spend more money. The app took the Priceless idea, long a TV staple, and allowed people to interact with it anywhere via mobile device. Exploiting the iPhone's GPS technology, the app allowed users to find and share recommendations for shopping, dining and entertainment based on their current location. "The insight was it's much easier for people to tell each other how to spend money—to share things to do—rather than a credit card company telling them."

"I like a simple brief; one page," says Evan Fry, co-founder of Victors & Spoils. "Personally I like to frame it as, what's the one thing you'd like the target take away from seeing the finished work? I like that question because it keeps people on track and, oddly, it frees you up. It forces you to think about [the consumer's] mindset. It's an efficient question."

Many creatives agree that over that years the briefing process has become a bigger than necessary production.

The briefing process does seem to take longer than it should, says former Saatchi & Saatchi New York chief creative officer Gerry Graf (who in April 2010 had announced he was exiting the agency to start his own shop). "People like to make big documents and presentations. Like, if you're getting briefed on Taco Bell you'll go to a Mexican restaurant or something and have the briefing. They're fancy when all you need is a sentence or two."

The Snickers "Not Going Anywhere for a While" campaign, says Graf, came from an account person, and the insight that Snickers

> *Go ahead and start thinking from the moment you know the problem. Don't lose weeks or months waiting for that "perfect" briefing document to land in front of you. We've thrown traditional process out the window and clients love that we want to start the wheels turning really early. In effect we've reclaimed the calendar, and with far more time to think and experiment the outcome is often dramatically better.*
>
> Nancy Vonk, co-chief creative officer
>
> of Ogilvy Toronto

wasn't competing against other candy bars, but against other snack-y, between-meal-type foods, like a slice of pizza or a bagel. "So we started writing scripts," says Graf, "and the first thing that came to our minds was, these guys were eating in a Chinese restaurant and they order sesame chicken. The waiter takes the order and we see the kitchen door open and six cats go running out. The idea was, 'not going to be eating for a while?' It started there. We showed the ECD at the time, Charlie Miesmer and he said, don't make it eating, just make it about the fact that you're going to be away from food for a while. That's when it changed to 'not going anywhere for a while.'"

BBDO's Greg Hahn boils the entire process down to the simplest of questions. "Someone told me once, and this has helped me more than anything in my career, write down on a piece of paper, 1: what to say, and 2: how to say it. That's it. That's advertising right there. I usually find that when there's a problem it's with number 1. You don't know what you're trying to say." Which comes, he says, from muddy, overwrought briefs. "Sometimes the brief has been designed by four or five people sitting around a table and everyone wants to put something in it and it ends up with too much thinking." The solution? "I step way from the meetings. I start thinking about what is the product or the problem, innately. Use intuition. Most of the time it's been overthought so much; step back, really see the thing."

Many creatives agree that getting the "what to say" part right is important, and has a lot to do with the brief and knowing what the strategy is. After that, usually, ideas flow a little more freely.

"You want to get under the skin of a problem up front; get to the truth of what you want to say about the brand, really kind of spend a lot of time up front getting to a really bulletproof strategy," says 180 Amsterdam ECD Sean Thompson, who says briefs tend to be a bit more open these days, but that the narrow brief is typically better. "When you get to the strategy, when you've gone through this stage where you go, OK, this is the right thing to say, then the ideas just happen."

First you have to be creative enough to engage the person to let you in, then you have to earn your keep by solving their problems, by coming up with things they're interested in. You have to earn your way in and then deliver.

Bill Wright, creative director

of Crispin Porter + Bogusky

DIGGING INTO THE PROBLEM:
RESEARCH—DEEP OR SHALLOW?

To determine how a brand can fit in with consumers' real lives and enter a conversation in a relevant way, it seems rather obvious that you should know your brand. The first step in any ad assignment is research. But how deeply you should know the brand in question is a matter of opinion among creatives.

While some copywriters like to retain some distance, the better to be able to view the brand as the consumer would, others immerse themselves in the brand and the company they're working with.

Given the potential scope of brand ideas today, it seems like the research-heavy way is a more relevant approach now, particularly for those who are newer to the game, and particularly for those who expect to be authoring creative solutions that transcend ads. When you are creating business solutions, it's a good idea to know about the business. This means not just knowing the product intimately, but knowing how it's distributed and sold, knowing its competitors and what kind of marketing they're doing and have done in the past, the market conditions that are affecting the company and the sector, how people have used and are using the product, and knowing about your brand's past ad campaigns.

"You read every scrap of info on the product you can find," says Wright. "I tell copywriters, once you know more than I do, you're ready to start."

Rick Condos, ECD at Goodby and one of the creatives behind two of the most award-winning campaigns in recent years, Coke's "Happiness Factory" and Doritos' "Hotel 626," calls himself a research junkie. "I think it's because I started out as an account person and the agency I grew up in, Weiss Whitten Stagliano, was really known for its strategic rigor. The more information I can have, the more I can work with people to understand the business, the more I think it unlocks my creativity. Everyone is different. Some people don't want to know anything, that's where they find the freedom. For me, the tighter the brief, the more information I have, the more I feel hemmed in, the better. That's the way something sparks and you find a new space for a product. It helps me understand the problem and it's all about problem solving."

ENABLE ROAMING

Several books about writing, including Luke Sullivan's *Hey Whipple: Squeeze This,* have emphasized some form of what you might call creative stewing, allowing the subconscious mind space and time to work its magic. Graf says as a writer he would go hard on the research and writing, but he also cited the power of subconscious problem solving.

"Reading *Zen in the Art of Writing* by Ray Bradbury, that's where I got my process from," says Graf. "He talked about doing as much research as possible then not doing anything for a while because your subconscious starts working. You're telling your subconscious the problem then you let things churn for a while. The actual writing is getting the solution out of your subconscious. That's really how it worked for me. When I was writing a TV idea or print ad or billboard, I'd always keep a pad with me. The majority of ideas would come after an entire day of working on the problem. Then on the walk home things would start popping out of my head."

WRITE, WRITE, WRITE. WRITE SOME MORE.

Have you ever given a speech in front of a large group of people? You probably found it helpful to read your speech aloud in an empty room or in front of your roommate or romantic partner beforehand. Note that just reading it to yourself, in your head, doesn't accomplish the same thing.

COPYWRITER'S TIP

COME TO GRIPS WITH PUBLIC SPEAKING

You may have gravitated toward writing because you don't like speaking, or you don't like people. In either case, it's likely you don't like speaking in front of people.

You will, unfortunately, have to speak. Whether for internal meetings, or client presentations or speaking at events, you will need to sort your presentation skills.

If you're the kind who doesn't even like yelling out your airline on the rental car shuttle bus, try one or more of the following:

Record yourself speaking. Watching a video of yourself or listening to an audio recording can be traumatic, but there's no better way of figuring out exactly what you're dealing with and then working to remove tics, tremors and tourettes-like vocal oddities.

Read *Confessions of Public Speaker* by Scott Berkun.

Take yoga and/or an acting class. Really. Yoga is about breathing and there is scarcely anything more essential when you're nervous and trying to form words. Breathing is a surprisingly prominent component of acting class, too, and, if you plan to be doing any commercials or other performance-based content, the perspective can only be helpful.

Be flexible. Don't take no for an answer, even from yourself. Be interesting. When you write something ask yourself, does it make me give a shit? If it doesn't, it isn't working.

Kash Sree, executive creative director

of Pereira & O'Dell

And so it is with writing. Thinking is great. By all means, think. But most copywriters will attest that magic happens when thoughts are manifest, when they travel from your brain through your fingers and keyboard and are committed to visual reality.

Condos calls it "writing your way to the answer." As a creative director, he says "people want you to give them the answer or they want to just have the idea and then start writing. I love what Steven King said in his book *On Writing;* he said that writing is like taking a walk in the woods and tripping over a bone. You take out your brushes and if you stay at it long enough you'll find the dinosaur. It takes time and patience and sheer volume of words. Anything I've written where it came down to a tag line, there were ten thousand words to get to that tag line. Pages and pages and brain dumps. I write a letter to myself almost; everyone has to find a way to write toward a problem instead of just thinking about it."

Graf says with each new project he would start a notebook. "I would just fill pages, writing down anything that came to mind when I thought about the product, I'd just write and not stop writing. You're taking a train of thought and then something pops out."

LET THE AUDIENCE TELL THE STORY, OR, SOMETIMES IT'S WHAT YOU DON'T SAY THAT COUNTS

Previous chapters have touched on the idea and given examples of copywriter as storyteller and have explored how the digital age has meant that the best stories are those that an audience can help tell, contribute to, and share.

This is an important thing to consider when it comes to sitting down and cracking a brief. Especially for writers who have come up in the full-service agency world, this can mean understanding that your best work might not be your "best writing" in the classic advertising sense.

"If you're a natural wordsmith, the transition is not so hard, when it comes to all the ways of applying copywriting to different media and circumstances," says Calle Sjoenell. "But it's more like, for those from a more 'traditional' background, you are trained to want to tell stories through your writing; you think, I want to write something to get into people's heads; I want to talk first. But, sometimes you should think of it as wanting people to talk for themselves." Says Pelle, "a lot of great communication happens in the audience's heads when they can figure out an ad or figure out a story or between clicks on a site. That's the second story you're writing; what happens in people's brains when they read. In between the lines is as important as what's in the lines."

Premutico calls it the ability to "say it without saying it. I've always believed that being a good writer is about what you don't say, and in that sense the best writing has always been interactive in nature, in the sense that you leave it to the audience to complete the story, and contribute their imagination. This is especially important in the land of advertising as it becomes more and more important to get your message across in a way that pulls people in."

Pelle Sjoenell sums up the creative's role as that of a story builder. "Being a storyteller to me is a brand telling a story. Story building is more a brand that wants to take people on a journey of building a story together. Whether it's a film or an interactive piece, you want to get people's own participation or thoughts into whatever you're doing."

COLLABORATE

Many agencies are experimenting with different creative team combinations, but some interpretation of Bernbach's copywriter/art director construct is actually still in effect at most agencies. In most full-service, and even in many digital agencies, some sort of team, whether it's a classic copywriter/art director pairing, or some variation (copywriter, interaction designer, etc.) is the central creative entity working on any given project. But in most cases, at some point the team expands to include other creative, tech, strategic and production voices.

"Interaction designers, user experience people, digital strategists, behavioral strategists, ethnographers, these are the people who are playing now and adding to the mix of the traditional copywriter and art director," says Lariu, who came to advertising from the digital world, as an interactive designer turned digital art director. She was paired with O'Rourke, who comes from the "traditional" advertising side.

In more and more instances, collaboration is the norm. When ideas started to transcend one platform and when idea and execution started to become more inextricably linked, the creative process began to demand a wider cohort of talents contributing to any one project.

Unsurprisingly, the Swedes have a particular knack for collaboration. The Sjoenell brothers say that when they joined BBH New York, they traded the two desks in their shared office for one big couch. "We put in a sofa so everyone can come in and work together. The Swedish way of working in groups and de-emphasizing ego, that's kind of proven to become something you have to do in general in the industry these days," says Pelle Sjoenell. "No one can be the expert in everything. You have to rely on a group of experts to get anything done. When it comes to teams, we work with one team and we trust them and work with them closely and then we allow others into that group—be it planners, media geniuses, technologists. It's not a one-man show."

A WORD ON ORIGINALITY

If you study advertising for long enough, you really gain appreciation for the sentiment, so ably articulated by Shakespeare, that "there be nothing new, but that which is / Hath been before." (Which, of course, was said before, in Ecclesiastes: "What has been will be again; what has been done will be done again; there is nothing new under the sun"). We live in a remix culture. Pick any of the best-known, most award-winning campaigns of the last several years, and you can find an online complaint that "that idea ran in Spain six years ago." But that's not a license for tired, lame ideas, and it's not an excuse for knowingly ripping off the ideas of other people.

The line between inspiration and larceny is a fine one, and it moves. You'll always have to use your own sense of creative integrity as a guide, but you can give it a head start by simply avoiding the chestnuts, the well-trodden path and the fallbacks.

Here are some. Just don't create any ads using these tropes and you'll be ahead of the game.

THE "THAT'S REFRESHING" TROPE

You know the drill: show an attractive woman watching the football game with her hand down her pants and belching. Add voice-over: "Now that's refreshing!" Just like [product here].

No. No it's not. It's the opposite of refreshing because we've seen in a trillion times. Move on. (Modifications of this include "Think this is [surprising, cool, cold, hot, wrong, etc.]? Then you should see [insert product or service attribute here].")

THE "I'M SO DISTRACTED BY THE AWESOME NATURE OF THE PRODUCT THAT I DIDN'T NOTICE [INSERT OUTRAGEOUS VISUAL PHENOMENON HERE]" DEVICE

A dog walks into a kitchen and whips up an omelet. Its owner says, in deadpan, "Wow, I've never seen that before," only he's looking at his cell phone bill or the new bottle his beer comes in, or something of that nature. Get it?

It worked when Volkswagen did it in a famous print campaign in the '90s. It won't ever work for you again. Keep trying.

THE "WOW THAT'S A REALLY INNOVATIVE TECHNIQUE I JUST SAW IN A FILM OR MUSIC VIDEO. I'M GOING TO MAKE AN AD AROUND IT COMPLETELY WITHOUT CONTEXT" MANEUVER

Remember the frozen moment from *The Matrix*? Yes, of course you do, even if you never saw the movie—because the technique was used relentlessly in commercials for years after.

This is a tricky one. As a copywriter, you're immersed in the wider world of culture, art, entertainment, technology. And the latest and greatest from that wider world can and should inform your work. As noted, it's hard to discern the line between influence and homage and gratuitous thieving.

Not long ago, BBDO Mexico caught hell for making a Snickers spot that, er, "borrowed" a little too liberally from the much-loved skate film *Fully Flared,* directed by Ty Evans, Cory Weincheque and the über-influential Spike Jonze. The film, created on behalf of Lakai Footwear, featured super slo-mo footage of skaters doing tricks on an array of exploding surfaces, accompanied by an atmospheric track from M83. The Snickers spot featured . . . well, it was exactly the same.

This is a bad idea. Either get Spike Jonze on board your project or think of something else.

THE "THINGS GOING BACKWARD" TECHNIQUE

Rewind. Start over.

THE "RUBE GOLDBERG MACHINE" METHOD

As of summer 2010, we can add this. Wieden + Kennedy London created one of the most talked-about ads of the decade with its 2003 spot, "Cog" for Honda. The epic ad featured an eye-popping chain-reaction sequence created with disassembled Honda parts. Of course, critics immediately cried foul, citing the 1987 film *The Way Things Go,* from Peter Fischli and David Weiss. Cog certainly borrowed from that film and from several other Goldberg contraption–themed sources. But the resulting spot felt fresh and inventive.

More recently, the band OK Go!, known for its elaborate, prone-to-virality-videos, used an over-the-top Rube Goldberg device in the promo for "This Too Shall Pass," sponsored by State Farm, and viewed over 15 million times on YouTube. The chain-reaction device has since been used several other times, to somewhat diminishing effect.

Let's leave it for now, shall we?

BE ORIGINAL, BUT MINE THE
GOLD THAT'S ALREADY THERE

As noted in previous chapters, the first brilliant move made by CP+B on behalf of Burger King was the resurrection of the chain's famous tag line, "Have It Your Way." There could scarcely have been a better overall identity for the brand in the era of consumer control. Other campaigns have similarly tapped the value in a brand's archive while offering something modern.

"I like to play off whatever equity a brand or product already has," says Gerry Graf. He harnessed a historical ad device in the famous Skittles work he did while at TBWA\Chiat\Day New York from 2003 to 2007. The marketer had, for several years, used the somewhat obvious but effective device of a rainbow in its ads for the colorful candies. When Graf took over the account, he knew the agency's new work would employ the rainbow, but in a more modern way. "We knew we wanted to do something with the rainbow—originally the campaign featured a little girl who would whisper, 'Taste the rainbow' at the end of the ads. In an early spot, we had a girl who went up to a guy on the street and whispered 'Look out for the car,' and he said 'What?' And she whispered 'Look out for the car,' and he said 'What??' and then eventually he got run over." That early interpretation of the existing Skittles sensibility would be further twisted over the years into a series of stellar ads, like "Touch" and "Piñata."

NO MORE DRAMA IS FINE FOR YOUR HOME LIFE.
AT WORK, IT'S ALL ABOUT DRAMA

There's a classic quote from French writer Gustav Flaubert that has been beaten to death on Facebook updates everywhere: "Be regular and orderly in your life that you may be violent and original in your work."

There are, of course, several delightful tales of ad men engaging in workplace violence over the years. British creative Graham Fink, now ECD at M&C Saatchi London once threw a plant across the room and broke a TV set when he was told he couldn't work with his chosen director, Tony Kaye, and later famously perched on a window ledge and threatened to leap in defense of his . . . creative integrity.

He was no doubt paying homage to madman George Lois, who in 1959 threatened to jump from a third-story window if a client didn't approve his campaign for Goodman's Matzos and who once over-turned a boss's desk for the crime of philistinism.

Perhaps in lieu of this sort of roughhousing, you can use drama.

Leo Burnett talked about the inherent drama in every product. In the 1940s he asked what would happen if you placed high-impact photos of red meat against a red background. Burger King's "King" character, with his big head and eerie plastic rictus delighted and hor-rified people in equal measure. Droga5 got some calls from Home-land Security because its 2006 "Still Free" spot for Ecko appeared to depict someone tagging Air Force One with graffiti.

It's easy to assume that in the advertising world, where everyone seems to be trying not to offend anyone, you'd want to steer clear of drama, tension. And many advertisers do in fact stay well away from it—their ads make up the 90 percent of skippable, forgettable and, ironically, in the end offensive work that no one bothers with.

Be a student of drama. "Storytelling and story arc, that can apply to anything that you're doing," says CP+B's Bill Wright. "You set up a conflict and then provide a resolution. Any piece of effective com-munication has to have that. I'm a fan of David Mamet and his defi-nition of drama is: the quest of our hero to overcome those things that prevent him from achieving his goal. If you can do that, you've got an audience. And that applies to interactive stuff too; the simplest billboard has tension to it and hopefully your product unlocks the tension."

SEEK THE TRUTH

Finding drama and storytelling, however, aren't the same as creating fiction around a product. The consumer-controlled, on-demand, so-cial, conversational world, as we've seen, is transparent. The notion of creating ads that represent an eye-rollingly large departure from what the product actually is, does and stands for seems anachronistic now. We've seen more and more examples of the painful public dissonance between a brand's ad fiction and reality. United, with its lyrical ads about the romance of flying crash-landed into a customer's highly publicized musical complaint about the airline's callous disregard for guitars and shoddy customer service. And perhaps nowhere is the advertising/reality gulf wider, and more downright criminal, than in the case of BP, a marketer that, through advertising, created the persona of an environmentally responsible, alternative-energy innovator when in reality it was just another powerful and astonishingly rich oil company that willfully flouted environmental safeguards at every opportunity for the sake of profits.

On a less tragic scale, in the old ad paradigm, products like beer and cars positioned themselves as part of a glamorous world full of nookie with women orders of magnitude more attractive than you are; household cleaning products were sold as key components to not just a clean floor, but a Zen-like personal satisfaction, the key to a woman's very self-worth.

The best advertising is built on a brand truth and also treats an audience with some degree of respect.

Paul Bennett, the chief creative officer of design powerhouse Ideo summed up the essential shift in *Ad Age*, asking, "Are you in the business of seeking truth and telling it, or of creating a myth and selling it?"

BBH New York CEO Kevin Roddy says the age of transparency will keep brands more honest. "The world is rapidly changing from an advertising environment where the brand speaks and the consumer simply listens, to one where the brand and the consumer interact, giving much power to consumers to understand the realities of a brand and its advertising," says Roddy. "And that's only going to increase with time. I think this dynamic will force more brands to stop making exaggerated claims and do simpler, authentic demonstrations. And as a result, it will force brands to spend more time making sure they have something relevant and important to demonstrate. In other words, this may force brands to improve. It will become less and less possible for inferior brands to outspend and outshine better products, and more possible for the best product to win."

THE BACK STORY—THE WRITING THE AUDIENCE DOESN'T SEE, BUT FEELS

Copywriters who have a hand in creating bigger, ongoing, integrated ideas are increasingly responsible for creating a structure or narrative underpinning for the work that the public sees, the back story that allows brand ideas to be played out in different media and to grow in different directions.

When CP+B took on Burger King and revived the Have it Your Way line, it also resurrected The King, who ruled, silently, smilingly, over much of the agency's work starting in 2004.

The King first showed up in commercials, but he also appeared in the agency's Sneak King video games, online and even in paparazzi snaps "leaked" to the tabloids.

Underlying much of the King-based work coming out of the agency was a narrative structure written by a copywriter. These were words that the public would never see, but that created the tone for the campaign and established a character portrait for The King.

"It's a major part of the copywriter's job now," says CP+B ECD Rob Reilly. "How do you maintain the brand voice across everything you're doing? We were very aware of that with Burger King and The King—we needed to know what his role was going to be in culture. We asked a copywriter to write the rules of The King—what can and can't he do? When you're creating intellectual property that represents your brand you have to know what the rules are. So, for The King, well, he's royalty, he'll throw the first pitch at baseball game, he doesn't talk ever, he doesn't interact with children—he's an adult king . . . As a campaign develops and you have things that are interacting with the consumer in different ways, you have to have rules of engagement. That usually falls on the copywriter."

Campfire's Mike Monello says the back story that is now a big part of writing for long form will become more important in advertising. "George Lucas is the ultimate master of this; in the Star Wars universe you get 27 volumes of just, like, Alliance logs. They created this whole bible of the universe so you understand the rules of the world when you put something out there and so other writers understand the background of the characters and what they've experienced in the past. We'll start to see this become more important as brands start to invest in narratives that live longer."

Rick Condos says the more elaborate back story or structural writing addresses "how do we take this new frontier and make sure we're putting craft into it. [At Goodby] our work looks a little more polished and feels more thought through. And to me that's where a good writer can really come in. It's not just writing headlines, it's writing an entire back story for this experience that's so interesting that even if I as a viewer don't ever know that, it affects the work I see in a way where it feels more thought out and feels more interesting."

That behind-the-scenes, deep-knowledge type of writing extends to more internal applications too. Creatives are not only charged with creating brand ideas that transcend media-specific communications, they are often responsible for bringing those ideas to life for clients.

"So much now the job of the copywriter is articulating ideas to clients that are difficult to articulate," says Reilly. "It's not a spot anymore, maybe it's a platform we're asking you to embrace, or, here's why you need to change the name of your car from Golf to Rabbit. So many clients are looking for narratives for their company. I say to writers if you can write a brand essence video you'll have a long career. It isn't easy."

Says Leo Premutico, "The writer's core function will remain similar, but the role the writer plays within the broader team is being redefined. A lot of the conversations out there are framed by the way a brand communicates. So writing in this sense is more important than it ever was, especially as we have the chance to react and adjust to that conversation taking place. It's also so crucial internally, when organizations are asked to understand and articulate who they are on so many more levels than they ever have been asked to do before. So the job has become more complex and demanding as creative agencies move away from simply offering advertising solutions and towards using creativity to offer business solutions."

DID WE MENTION: KNOW HOW TO WRITE!

Most creative directors interviewed in these pages cited the rise of student books packed with "ideas," with no commensurate density of good, solid writing.

Maybe there's a craft gap, maybe there isn't. Maybe we do live in an age when good enough is good enough.[6] Maybe creatives who came up in the "traditional" world are lamenting a notion of and a perspective on craft that was specific to that media era, in other words, in the era of the million-dollar TV spot, which was, frame for frame, more expensive than a movie and more lovingly produced.

It's hard to know. But what is known is that great idea people who are also great writers will always have an edge at agencies. You may be a technology geek, you may have great desktop production skills, you might be a crack strategist and business nerd, but if you're calling yourself a writer, you should be a strong writer first; you should be reading all you can and writing for all you're worth. If doing that doesn't appeal to you, maybe you should pursue some other creative path.

Working on the craft of writing is not something that will ever be a wrong answer. The way the industry is evolving, you may find yourself writing something completely different as your career progresses.

CHAPTER 6

LIFE IN ADLAND

For a while there, not too long ago, it wasn't hard to find creative directors and other ad types of a certain vintage who were fond of telling all those who would listen that things were better back in the day. Ads were better, creatives were better, there were more *characters*. You could identify most of these nostalgia merchants by their dress and overall personal appearance—that vague look of having been stuck in time sartorially.

The "they don't make ads like they used to" argument is wrong headed, of course. As discussed previously, ads weren't better, across the board, back in whatever your idea of the golden ad age was. Yes, there have been times and places of particular creative fecundity—Bernbach's DDB at the top of its powers in the early '60s, Cliff Freeman in the '80s and '90s—that did cause a tide that lifted creativity in general. But everything didn't stop after they did; the best people built on what they had created and made their own gains.

There was the same overall ratio of great to good to bad advertising then (whenever then was) as now. If you're skeptical about this, go back and watch all the Super Bowl spots from a selection of years pre-1990. Not just the famous spots, all the spots in the game—archives are easy to find online. Not exactly a parade of 1984s and Mean Joe Greens, eh?

In commercials, as in most everything else, things just tend to improve and evolve to reflect the increasing sophistication and changing sensibilities of an audience and a culture.

So, remembering when is just not a great attitude to guide your life in general, and it's certainly not the ideal way to guide a creative department and mentor new creatives.

But one could hardly blame these guys. They had it pretty good in advertising's TV age. That's not to say it wasn't—isn't—an extremely challenging job, with grueling hours and soul-curdling moments of existential crisis. In fact, the long hours have been one of the (lame) excuses proffered to explain the dearth of women in senior creative positions—the time demands are such that you can forget about scheduling things like babies. And as for the frustration factor, when Luke Sullivan outlines in *Hey Whipple* some of the different subspecies of clients a creative may run into in the course of a career, it seems like he's being nice.

But being an agency creative isn't roughnecking or coal mining either. The compensation has been, until now at least, ample and the perks many. Up until very recently, when the head of a digital agency wanted to lampoon traditional advertising's lumbering inefficiencies and tragic disengagement from reality, he would paint a picture of a creative divo who, having written a script for a big-budget, effects-laden spot, flew first-class to L.A. to shoot with a temperamental genius director and enjoy a week (at least) at the posh Shutters on the Beach in Santa Monica.

The wistful lookers-back are referred to in the past tense because most of them are gone from the business now. It's just too challenging and too exciting a time for those who are simply clinging to the glory days with failing hands and waiting to cash out, for those who aren't excited about the possibilities of now. For those who aren't in it, as they say, to win it.

And so, do we refer to the sweet copywriting gig as an artifact of history too? Is the heyday of advertising over? Will you ever swaddle your sweet behind in a Shutters bathrobe?

It is the opinion put forward in this book and of nearly all of the people quoted in it that this time period, right now, is as much of a heyday as the ad and marketing industry has ever seen and that it is potentially the most exciting time to be a creative person.

That's not to say it's not a scary time; the industry is at a complete crossroads. The whole model that has given the industry and copywriters their basic set of operating assumptions has crumbled.

I don't believe in the good old days; the good old days are here

now if you work hard and care enough. The difference between

a great ad and a good ad is the amount of time you're prepared

to spend on it, the care you're prepared to give it.

David Abbott, copywriting legend

and co-founder of U.K. agency

Abbott Mead Vickers BBDO

Perhaps a fitting if slightly terrifying comparison would be journalism. Until digital technology—the web and blogging software—put the power to disseminate words in the hands of everyone, news, information and opinion were written by professional journalists who worked for media organizations. Now, of course, news, information, opinion, photography and other content are supplied by everyone who wants to supply them, for fun or profit. In the economic downturn of 2008–2009, that basic shift resulted in a magazine and newspaper die-off that took even the cynical media elites by surprise.

News organizations still exist, obviously, but they are typically more streamlined beasts, and their future is not exactly clear. In a May 2010 piece on the sale of news institution *Newsweek, New York Times* columnist David Carr asked, "How can it be that Associated Content, a content farm that has zero brand recognition, went for a reported $100 million this month to Yahoo, yet Newsweek, a huge part of the national conversation since its founding in 1933, might be valued at less than zero? It's a cold fact of economic life that the value of a business is an expectation of future growth. If Associated Content will deliver 15 percent annual growth in earnings and Newsweek offers only compounding losses, the smart money will forgo the admired publishing enterprise led by a Pulitzer Prize winner, and instead opt for a business of link-bait stories churned out by people you've never heard of."[1]

While many believe that the fall of institutionalized journalism is a calamity that has serious repercussions for the idea of democracy, others believe that the rise of citizen journalists and the explosion of news blogs have meant a different but more robust system of information distribution.

And so, in the ad world, where there was formerly one basic apparatus for the creation and delivery of ads, now there are many. Where only certain people were able to create and distribute videos and other compelling content to large audiences, now anyone can potentially do so.

And then there was the little matter of economic Armageddon.

In the 2008–2009 economic shitstorm, many agencies downsized; according to a report in *Ad Age*, from December 2007 to June 2009, the industry shed over 163,000 jobs.[2] The holding company WPP alone laid off 14,000 people in its agencies, but even many smaller shops cut headcounts. And of course some agencies just closed down—including the legendary Cliff Freeman & Partners, the New York shop that produced some of the TV era's most famous ads and most famous copywriters. Most agree that even as the ad industry picks up, the jobs aren't coming back, or at least not all of them. Advertising, like every other industry, is and will likely continue to be a leaner, and sometimes meaner, affair, with more people doing more with fewer resources.

Meanwhile, marketers look to an increasing array of creative solutions and creative partners to help them connect their brands with people. The Big Advertising Agency is no longer the only entity that can claim exclusive ownership of the client relationship or claim to be the only place to get creative ideas to build brands.

Over the last several years, we've seen more marketers unmoor themselves from longstanding monogamous relationships with big agencies and begin cherry picking creative partners. This practice transcends the traditional creative/media/digital division of agency labor. For years, clients would have a main "full service" or creative agency and then work with other companies for media buying, or for "below the line" specialties like direct, promotions and PR, and, later, for digital. But the agency splits are no longer necessarily along media/discipline lines; that is, marketers may be working with several agencies with the same offering, in the same competitive set. Coke has been the classic (sorry) example of a giant marketer that was once

affiliated with one giant agency and is now working with an assortment of agencies around the world. More recently, Harley Davidson
and its agency of 31 years, Minneapolis' Carmichael Lynch, announced their separation; Harley said it would not hold a review to
replace its agency of record as its communications would be handled
by an existing roster of shops.

Of course, that AOR relationship still exists. But more and more
agency executives are reporting that it's often a more promiscuous
arrangement.

So, to start the discussion of what the copywriter's role and life
are like in an agency, we have to back up and question the first assumption—the assumption of the agency.

WE DON'T NEED NO STINKING AGENCY

Among the brand creativity players that have expanded the scope of
their offering and, in some cases, taken a bigger share of client mind,
if not budget, are:

DIGITAL PRODUCTION COMPANIES

When marketing moved online, these were the companies that started
out helping full-service agencies produce banners and web sites.
Companies like The Barbarian Group were built on the technical pro-
ficiency required to make ideas like Subservient Chicken come to life.
In many cases, as the industry has evolved and digital has become
more central to any marketing plan, these companies have increased
the scope of their offering. With the growth of digital creativity, idea
and execution became more intertwined; digital production companies often had the answer to how to realize new ideas, often in a more
efficient manner than could be done at giant agencies. The natural
next step was to do more work directly with clients.

In November 2009, *Ad Age* reported that Wrigley had taken its
business from its digital agencies of record Tribal DDB, Digitas and
Agency.com and moved it to a consortium made up of Big Spaceship,
Firstborn and EVB, all companies that would have been considered
smallish digital production companies up to that point.[3] Whatever
the reason was for the move, the conclusion drawn by the industry

was extrapolated from general industry trends—brands looking to streamline their marketing process were favoring nimble over big and digitally driven over TV-legacy.

COMMERCIALS PRODUCTION COMPANIES

In 1999, than-six-year-old @radical.media was one of the industry's biggest and best-known production companies and, like every other production company, made its living—and a nice living at that—from making TV commercials. But even in 1999, Radical partners Jon Kamen and Frank Scherma were talking about expanding the scope of brand storytelling beyond 60 seconds and into new platforms. They were early adopters. In 2001, Radical worked with Wieden + Kennedy Portland on one of the earliest high-profile branded-content initiatives, *Nike Battlegrounds,* an MTV show about street basketball. The companies teamed up for other content projects like the documentary on Lance Armstrong's 2001 Tour de France win, *Road to Paris.* Radical has gone on to produce and create a platform-spanning range of content, working with ad agencies, media companies and directly with marketers. Its projects have spanned feature films (the documentary *Metallica: Some Kind of Monster,* Errol Morris's *The Fog of War,* the controversial and critically acclaimed Joe Berlinger documentary *Crude*), events (Concert for George, the Hardbat Classic, a ping-pong event produced with ESPN and K-Swiss), TV (Radical produced *In the Heights: Chasing Broadway Dreams,* based on the hit Broadway show), integrated campaigns and innovative digital projects like The Johnny Cash Project, a crowd-sourced video experiment created by Radical director Chris Milk and Google's data visualization whiz kid Aaron Koblin.

So what kind of company is this? Radical, like most production players, has shied away from the moniker "agency," partly because the company has for so long been a partner to agencies and isn't keen to muddy those waters, and partly because the handle doesn't quite fit. Radical calls itself a "a global transmedia company." In the last several years, other production companies have expanded their range; commercials shop Tool expanded into digital content, re-cruiting some of the biggest names in the digital production world, like indie game developer Jason Rohrer, Flash guru Grant Skinner and Papervision founder Carlos Ulloa; Smuggler, an A-list commercials shop, now has projects in development ranging from feature films to a Broadway show.

MEDIA COMPANIES

The other side of the network agency coin is Big Media—the huge media-buying and planning operations that were unbundled from creative agencies in the early '90s, companies like WPP's MindShare, IPG's Mediabrands and Omnicom's OMD. In a world where media is everything, not just a handful of channels, who better to take over the primary brand relationship than media companies, which could in some cases also claim a more sophisticated understanding of different parts of the consumer equation—like data—that became more important in the digital age?

As the digital revolution roiled the industry and shook up traditional roles, different entities tended to become territorial about who "owns" the client relationship, about who can take that 3 A.M. call from a CMO. Nowhere was the pissing contest more marked than between creative agencies and media companies. The latter have expanded their own scope, and some of them have pointedly added "traditional" creative directors and other full-service agency skills to round out their expertise and their offering to marketers.

But it's not just that kind of media company that fancies itself an all-round brand partner now. The media owners have also retooled. Obviously, these media players—production, publishing and distribution conglomerates (think Time Warner, Viacom, etc.)—have content creation and distribution cornered; now they are looking to round out their brand-building skills.

With client/agency relationships shifting and marketers turning more of their attention and resources to creating entertainment beyond the 30-second-spot framework, the entertainment industrial complex has taken a greater interest in talent from the ad world.

The entertainment industry, like any other, has undergone an involuntary belt tightening. TV ad revenues were once a vast, seemingly bottomless pool. With the aforementioned changes in the media landscape, that pool, while still enormous, isn't quite as deep as it used to be. And it's getting a little shallower and a little chillier every day. Of course the downside to arbitrarily slapping a brand on an entertainment property is that the entertainment part of that equation often falls down. Ham-fisted attempts at branded content have brought down the wrath of audiences and critics and have generally failed.

But media companies, like everyone else, have realized that if a brand is integrated into a program in a way that serves the audience first, everyone wins. This usually means bringing the brand thinking into the creative process at the earliest stages rather than jamming a brand into a property where it doesn't belong.

More and more, Hollywood and the media companies that run film and TV production and distribution companies and print publishers, and marketers in possession of multimillion-dollar budgets that were once devoted to buying media time for TV and print campaigns are uniting to figure out a better way. And many media companies are bringing brand-creative expertise in house.

In the earlier days of the digital revolution, many of these huge media companies appeared to be asleep at the switch or in some deep state of denial. Magazine powerhouse Condé Nast seemed so cocksure about the eternal power of print that it did little to translate the awesome brand equity of titles like *Vogue* into anything beyond big fat September issues. TV networks watched their audience numbers fall consistently over the last 15 years, and yet when upfront time[4] rolled around, they demanded ever-higher rates from the marketers buying airtime on their shows.

Now many media companies are catching up, investing in digital platforms and, in many cases, looking to work more closely with brands to integrate their messages into content and to create bespoke creative solutions.

Rather than acting merely as a distribution channel for advertising, they, like many other players, are looking for ways to partner effectively with brands up front, helping marketers shape their messages, which has, of course, long been the job of the ad agency.

Condé Nast's digital division has abandoned the pretense of not mowing traditional agency grass with the expansion of its in-house creative-services group, CND Studios. In 2010 *Ad Age* reported that the group was offering ad-making services to advertisers—even those not running in Condé Nast properties.

Under the CND banner, the publisher has done projects for the likes of Kenneth Cole, creating an online video series for the brand that ran on the company's website and on Facebook and YouTube. Other publishing companies have bulked up their in-house marketing services groups. Meredith, the publisher of "women's" magazines like *Better Homes & Gardens, Parents* and *More,* acquired digital/mobile shop The Hyperfactory, adding to the other companies it has purchased since 2006: interactive shops O'Grady Meyers and Genex, viral marketing shop New Media Strategies, health-care agency Big Communications, and analytics shop Directive.

NBC Universal in May 2010 announced the appointment of former agency creative director Andrew Ault as vice president and executive creative director in charge of integrated sales marketing. Ault, who had been a copywriter and creative director at agencies like Fallon, JWT and Crispin Porter + Bogusky, had always leaned to the content-creation side, creating music videos and working for a spell at CAA before joining NBC.

The media company is absorbing the brand know-how that was once the exclusive province of agencies, and combining it with its undeniable strengths in content production and distribution. "Brands are increasingly spending more time, and money, in the network/media space beyond just traditional ad buys," says Ault. "Additionally, whereas NBC was once a single network, NBC Universal is a company of multiple entertainment properties. So there's a need to have someone at NBC Universal who understands both brands and their marketing needs as well as the entertainment space. My role is to think of all sorts of ways for NBC Universal and brands to work together. Anything from branded content to show integrations to different ways of thinking about traditional ad spends."

There are smaller media players, too, that are providing new expertise to marketers and an interesting new approach to integrating brands and content. *Vice,* the youth culture magazine launched in Canada in 1996, has expanded its empire over the years to include music, film, books, retail stores and the online channel VBS.tv. The company was built on the back of the kind of absolute youth cred that comes with publishing stories like "Grandma Blowjob" and "Interview with a Black Guy"[5] and has somehow translated that core expertise into creating youth-focused brand initiatives for the likes of Nike, Red Bull, Dell and Intel.

In 2006 *Vice* launched a branding arm (an agency, effectively) called Virtue, which has since created a range of work for brands including brand ID, package design and ads for MTV/EA's Rock Band, a video series on mountain gorillas for Edun, and a technology and culture series called "Motherboard" for Dell. Recently, the unit worked with Intel on "The Creators Project," a web-based project that celebrates leading-edge artists and also includes a series of global events.

While Virtue has its own staff of creatives and brand experts, it also harnesses *Vice*'s existing and considerable talent base—a huge global group of young writers, photographers and graphic designers—for brand projects.

"We've been marketed to our whole lives, making our bullshit detectors very sophisticated," *Vice* co-founder Shane Smith told *Creativity*. "So our whole modus operandi was not to bullshit. We decided to set up this separate wing that could leverage our talent but also be a separate company to help brands reach this demographic."

"We believe that every brand must think and act like a media company," says Spencer Baim, who co-founded Virtue after having worked as an ad agency strategist. "This means, talking to your consumer (or audience) constantly in a manner that is welcomed. You want people to tune into your brand, not to push a message out. This completely changes the role of the copywriter; they literally become the voice of the brand, be it via a tweet, a magazine the brand produces, a content-rich website and on and on. The copywriter must also realize that the conversation now goes two ways, allowing the consumer to talk to the brand and the brand back to the consumer; the copy writer is that voice too. It is more malleable and more real."

Talent giant CAA has spent years building its brand detail. CAA's ties with the marketing world go back to 1991, when the agency famously plucked adland's shiniest gem—ad duties for Coca-Cola—out of the grasp of McCann Erickson and created the "Always" campaign, which introduced to the ad canon the now-legendary CG polar bears. The marketer eventually exited the agency but boomeranged in 2000 and became the inaugural client of the new CAA Marketing. This time, the iconic advertising move was to put Coke glasses in the hands of *American Idol* judges. The marketing unit also forged a successful Coke tie-in with the first two Harry Potter movies.

CAA bulked up its marketing unit in 2006, bringing on Ault as well as Jae Goodman, a copywriter and creative director who had served at agencies like Wieden + Kennedy and Publicis & Hal Riney.

As Goodman tells it, he was spending all of his non-billable time in his last agency gig trying to get different kinds of content projects off the ground. But such projects, though gaining more interest from marketers, were hard to execute. "Whether it's a videogame, a feature film or concert series, those things were incredibly cumbersome to create within the confines of a traditional agency simply because of the number of phone calls it takes. It took six months on one client I worked with at Riney, but here, I literally walk down the hall."

Goodman says he devoted so much time to non-ad projects while in the ad agency world "because it was fun, on one hand, but on the other hand we knew we were exercising a muscle we knew we'd need."

When he joined CAA, Goodman described his job as "wonderfully ambiguous and open to wild collaboration. I could collaborate with an ad agency, a production company, a publishing company, a concert pro-moter, a music artist, all to create something new, a new connection between consumers and the brand we represent. CAA has a great team of executives now, great creative minds, and they represent what I've been calling the biggest creative department in the world. All of a sud-den the world of possibilities is blown wide open for clients."[6]

From his office in the imposing glass and concrete edifice affec-tionately known as the Death Star, Goodman described the impor-tance of writing at CAA as, in part, being able to articulate ideas internally and to marketers. A portion of the end product of CAA Marketing's efforts is written by others—screenwriters, TV writers, etc. But Goodman says writers are essential in not just creating but ex-plaining new ideas. "If you're doing the first-ever live interactive show, you have to be able to explain what it is, what it means for production, how consumers are going to interact with it, everything about it. We create presentations just to be able to create these platforms. Your ability to describe things succinctly is as important now internally as it ever was externally."

AND THEN THERE'S GOOGLE

As if Google weren't a dominant enough force in every other area of human endeavor, in 2007 the company launched Google Creative Lab, whose mandate, boiled down to its gritty essence, is "to do epic shit."

Creative Lab ECD Robert Wong, who delivered that pithy mission statement, elaborates: "The Google Creative Lab is a small team that strives to re-think marketing across every kind of media—currently existing or not, with Google as its sole client. Our mission is 'to re-mind the world what it is that they love about Google.' Our job is to manage and steward the Google brand, find new ways to communicate the company's innovations, intentions and ideals, and do work of which we can all be immensely proud. We want people ambitious and crazy enough to think we can actually change the world."

Wong was a former accountant and then graphic designer who did a stint in the agency world and then as a creative director at Starbucks before being recruited by Lab employee number one, managing director Andy Berndt, himself a copywriter turned creative director and then managing director at Ogilvy before joining Google. The Creative Lab employs 50 people from a range of disciplines—design, writing, coding—but all of them are united by their, um, "Googlyness," something that Wong translates as, yes, smart and multitalented but also "ambitious, humble and altruistic, but also with a sense of scale, like you feel like you can impact a LOT of people with your work."

Wong looked for those qualities in the Google Five, a handful of students recruited to come and work at Google for a year and then go unto the ad industry and lead by example. The 2009 Five scored one of the most high-profile ad coups of all—a Super Bowl spot. All the more impressive given that Google has never run a Super Bowl spot, isn't known for doing traditional advertising, and has senior executives who have sworn never they'd never do TV commercials and have said, in public, that advertising was "the last bastion of unaccountable spending in corporate America."

The spot, called "Parisian Love," was a simple counterpoint to the typical broadly comedic, big-budget, lowest-common-denominator formula trotted out by the majority of advertisers in the game. The ad simply framed the classic Google search bar and told the story of a blossoming romance through a series of searches being typed by an unseen suitor, who begins by typing "study abroad paris" and ends with "how to assemble a crib."

The Google Five, whose ranks include two writers, two designers and a programmer, didn't create the spot for the Super Bowl; it was a video the team had done as part of a bigger brief on search. The team had been looking at new ways to let people know about different ways search could be used, but also to "remind people what they love about Google search," says Wong. "It's a very logical tool but there's a lot of emotion behind it. We started thinking along the lines of, if each search is representative of a moment in your life, or an interest, or something you're pursuing, then if you view a certain combination of those in a linear fashion then it becomes almost like a snapshot of that moment in your life," says Tristan Smith, one of the writers in the group. "All of a sudden it's like a short film clip or a string of photos; you can see a short biography of that person."

Says Smith, "Robert had used the line, the best results don't show up on a search engine, they show up in your life. If you look at a photograph, you don't think about that moment you had the camera in your hand and pressed the shutter, you think about what the photo is, what happened when it was taken. That's what searches are representing."

But maybe even more significant than the work they produced was the way of working the Five learned at Google, which is perhaps an exemplar of how creatives will be working more and more in the agency world.

Naturally, that way is open, iterative and collaborative in the extreme.

"There's very little screen privacy," laughs Google Fiver Anthony Cafaro. "Even within the group, it wasn't ever like 'this is my thing, this is your thing.'" Says Smith, "I think ad school trained you a lot of the time to be very competitive, like there's a kind of killer instinct they try and create. Here it didn't make sense to try and compete against everyone all the time; it felt like everyone was working on one thing and trying to do the best work. It was more about everyone doing their best to lift each other up."

The Creative Lab works on a range of communications assignments with a large number of agencies. Wong says if there's a Google way that could be transplanted to the agency world, it would be about "more listening, less talking; more feeling, less thinking; more doing, less promising; more inventing, less polishing."

There are other brand-creativity entities, including those that haven't been invented yet.

And of course there are digital agencies, which more and more transcend their description and act as agencies of record for marketers.

In the meantime, there are other players outside of the creative agency/production template that are, or are perceived to be, expanding the scope of their offering to marketers.

Management consulting companies—like McKinsey—seem to lurk like evil specters around the margins of advertising, and they figure in the spooky campfire tales told by agency execs. The classic scenario has full-service ad agencies ceding control of the primary brand relationship, the strategic reins if you will, to a McKinsey, which would manage the big-brand picture and then apportion specific executional duties to ad agencies and others. The ad agency then becomes sort of a production company, making a certain kind of communications product but having no control over the direction of the brand.

It's a scenario that's haunted the dreams of agency CEOs. But it hasn't happened. Yet.

But as marketers look to streamline their operations and cut costs while trying to find new ways to connect with audiences, they are questioning basic assumptions, like the one that says a big agency network must handle their business. Even global marketers, which would typically default to an agency network with offices around the world, are looking at different options, including the option of zero agency. It's not unreasonable to predict more marketers bringing more strategic and creative functions in house, and tapping specialists to execute a range of ideas.

All that said, don't count out ad agencies as we know them just yet. While the industry did for a long time seem better at talking about new ways of doing things rather than doing things new ways, in the last few years there have been exceedingly interesting things happening at agencies, both full service and digital. Many agencies have developed expertise in delivering the things that marketers would have typically gone to a specialized company to do.

Several agencies, including BBH, JWT and Wieden + Kennedy have significant branded-content initiatives to their credit. CP+B has been developing an industrial design practice and created a bike-sharing program that's now up and running in Denver. Many agencies have started developing their own intellectual property, their own products ranging from a line of cosmetics (Anomaly, New York) to a gourmet hot dog restaurant (Mother, New York) and chocolate and coconut water brands (The Brooklyn Brothers).

Why should you care about the fate of agencies, or which entities end up doing what kind of work for which marketers? Unless you're an agency owner, you shouldn't necessarily. The point here is to emphasize that the industry is in transition right now. There are basic assumptions (creatives work at ad agencies) that are still very much in place and could well be in place for years to come. But there's a bit of chaos swirling too. No one can say with certainty right now what the ad landscape will look like even in the near future. There is no right answer, and, as the Dread Pirate Roberts says, anyone who says differently is selling something.

But we're getting ahead of ourselves. If you're getting out of ad school, or deciding to flee from journalism right now in favor of the ad world, and you plan on joining an agency or creative shop of some description, what can you expect?

HOW COPYWRITERS ARE WORKING NOW

If there are any two words used in these pages and in the industry that most tidily sum up the change in how creatives work now, they are: increased collaboration.

While many agencies still employ some version of the art director/copywriter team, on most projects, at most agencies, that team at some point expands to include creative technologists, user experience and other designers, producers and an array of other contributors.

"When you're having such a vast conversation it absolutely requires collaboration," says Susan Credle, chief creative officer at Leo Burnett USA. "That was one of the significant changes that I've seen from the '90s to now. In the '90s, writers and art directors worked together alone and we locked our doors and our filing cabinets at night. Today, the best people that I'm around are collaborative, they want to share their work."

Many digital agencies have a more organic collaborative model because they don't have the legacy of the writer/art director team arrayed around a TV spot, and because things like user experience and utility have been a more entrenched part of their offerings. Says AKQA's Inamoto:

AKQA doesn't have set teams made up of copywriters working with the same art directors all the time. Part of the reason for this is the diversity of work we do. It's no longer just "campaigns" or "ads." User experience is a discipline that we embrace within our agency. . . . We think of this as part of the creative department. Depending on the nature of our relationship with our clients or the type of engagements or assignments we have, our team structure changes. Sometimes, it's the traditional model, but often it's not. It could be a visual designer and an user experience designer. It could be a user experience designer and a technologist. What we do as an agency is to create something that is delightful but also usable and useful. Put another way, what we do is about delivering an emotional story combined with a functional value. I have this new equation: the idea = emotion x function. So, I'm looking at partnerships between a copywriter and an user experience designer.

Dave Bedwood, creative partner at U.K.-based digital agency Lean Mean Fighting Machine, sums up the talent arrangement around a recent integrated campaign, "The Photographic Adventures of Nick Turpin": "The team structure had a writer, programmer, producer, account manager, photographer—Nick Turpin—and that was the core team. We try and keep the teams as small as possible; they need to be flexible and you can't have 18 people in umpteen meetings to make something good. I suppose a good barometer is that the Beatles were never more than four men and George Martin; they didn't get bigger to be more creative. If it's good enough for them, it's good enough for us!"

Mike Hughes, chief creative officer of The Martin Agency, creator of the Geico cavemen and the UPS white board guy and many other culturally impactful campaigns, says:

> On the most obvious level, we're shaking up the sacred one writer–one art director team. That's because we're asking more of these people than ever before. We're asking not just for ad ideas, but for broad-based creative platforms. Now in addition to traditional advertising conceptual thinking, we're asking our teams to give us both design thinking and digital thinking. So when we surround a problem today, there might be a creative technologist and a designer and a planner and a media planner (or two) and a producer (or two) in addition to the core writer/art director/creative director team. We're also giving our creative people more opportunities to direct, to produce, to develop new skills. (One of our writers created some charming hand-made dolls for one of our presentations. No kidding.)

Hughes says the agency is pushing to create a culture and a repertoire that act as a magnet for the best people across creative and
strategic disciplines; part of that involves making it a priority to develop creative projects outside of a strict ad mandate.

> We want to develop ideas, products and strategies that reach be-
> yond traditional advertising—because the best creative and strate-
> gic people are often eager to exercise their skills in different ways
> and in different venues. Sometimes we develop business solutions
> that have nothing to do with marketing or advertising. Sometimes
> we develop content that's branded for one of our clients—and
> sometimes we develop content that's just (hopefully) great content.
> Sometimes we take on causes just because we want to make the
> world a better place.
>   We'll soon be announcing a partnership with an Academy
> Award–nominated animation/production company to create a mu-
> sical show that will hopefully air next year. One of our copywriters
> developed the idea and the script, another is writing the songs. The
> wechoosethemoon.org site we created last year for the Kennedy Li-
> brary and AOL: for the writer and art director on that project, it
> was always much more about the library's educational mission than
> it was about marketing or advertising. We learned a lot from our
> Cavemen adventure with ABC—including a lot of things not to do.
> We're also taking on some serious causes—and we're tackling those
> issues without advertising. This is the most exciting time since the
> 1960s to be a copywriter.

The Barbarian Group's Rick Webb says the new creative team
comes with challenges, including the challenge of expanding the definition of who and what a creative lead is.

"I think there's a lot of talk about the burgeoning team size–
creative lead, tech lead, user experience lead, content strategist, social
media lead, community moderator, editor, producer, strategist, account director, account executive–along with the usual historic creative team–creative director, art director, designer, editor, screenwriter,
game designer," says Webb. "The challenges are managing teams that
large." He says TGB has a number of mechanisms for doing so.
Among them: "identifying a 'project lead' that has ultimate authority;
recognizing that it could be ANY of these leads—not necessarily de-
faulted to the creative director. Different projects have different aspects that lead—content, humor, design, tech, usability—that
necessitate explicitly making one lead dominant. And recognizing

that a great idea on the internet can be anything—an app, a comic, a video, a game, a blog—and that all of the team members can contribute to finding the best approach and thinking up the 'creative approach' and thus making the creative lead more of a shepherd and gatherer of ideas from the entire team rather than dictating or coming up with the ideas on their own." In the case of The GE Show, says Webb, the company's Flash developer conceived the game and co-wrote the site, and developers contributed editorial ideas. "I think the major insight, is removing the presumption that the creative lead is the main person responsible for executing the brief. Sometimes it's the developer, sometimes it's the information architect."

Kevin Roddy, chief creative officer at BBH New York also says that creatives in that (full-service) shop are working "less linearly. More fluidly. More collaboratively. In bigger teams and smaller teams. Some with success, and some as miserable failures," he says.

Says Roddy, "The walls of creativity are coming down in many instances. They need to. Idea ownership needs to be spread around. 'Creative teams' are being redefined. Reorganized. 'Creatives' need to see others as creative, as having the ability to help with an idea. They can't wall it off and only let a select few inside. The importance of the creative mind in advertising is still as important as it has ever been. Creativity is still an economic multiplier. So, in my opinion, we must all continue to celebrate those people in this business that make creativity the top of this industry's pyramid. Because it is those people that will drive us into the future. We just need to understand that there will be more and different kinds of these people from now on . . . and be comfortable with that."

Those "others," always a key part of the creative process at any agency, are becoming more important to and working more closely with creatives.

Who are these others?

THESE ARE THE PEOPLE
IN YOUR NEIGHBORHOOD

A copywriter's creative process is informed by the agency people who, traditionally, have not been considered part of the "creative department." But we know that traditional considerations tend not to apply in the post-digital world, and delineations between who is "creative" and who isn't are among the lines that have been smudged by the fingers of progress.

Here are some of your new creative partners and what they do.[7] In all cases, if they're good, they will make your work and your life better, if not easier. If they're bad, well, maybe your creative director will keep them out of your way.

THE ACCOUNT MANAGER

The account manager, well, manages accounts and client relationships. The account man caricature is that of the smooth schmoozer, the suit. Depending on the person, the role and the agency, this person possesses a mix of strategic smarts, diplomacy, a grasp of the big marketing picture, a grasp of the smaller project-management picture and sales savvy. In recent years, the account management function has come under scrutiny; as agencies moved toward a more streamlined, creative-forward offering, account management was seen by some as an unnecessary layer, and some agencies, like Mother, operate without the role. In a recent *Ad Age* piece on the plight of account managers, one exec noted that "At a lot of places, [the role has] devolved into basically a professional golf partner or lunch buyer."[8]

"Traditionally, account people were part salesman part account handlers," says account guy turned TBWA CEO Tom Carroll. "The very best had good marketing instincts and their clients' confidence. Good creative people always saw the value in strong account people, weak creatives never did. It was a pretty straightforward job. Today the best account people are more like Hollywood producers. There's so many parts of the media mix, and good account people have to know the role of each aspect from the ads to PR, social media and promotion."

THE ACCOUNT PLANNER

Though the philosophy behind account planning was alive in all the great agencies dating further back, it's widely held that planning as a discrete job description was "invented" in the 1960s in London by Stephen King (no, not that one) of JWT and Stanley Pollitt of Boase

Massimi Pollitt (BMP). It was imported to the United States in the early '80s by Chiat\Day founder Jay Chiat.

Essentially, account planners are the people who work to develop the strategic approach that underlies any brand communications. They are the experts in research, data and consumer behavior. They help form the insights that creatives work from.

Planner Henrick Habberstad called account planning "the creativity behind the creativity." He said:

> The planner plays an important role in creating a sensitive and deeper understanding of human behavior—what we call insight. In other words, the planner makes sure that a deeper, holistic understanding of consumer attitudes and reactions are brought to bear at every stage of advertising development (both strategy and creative). As the agency catalyst, the planner is a fully integrated member of the brand/account team, working closely together with the account manager, the copywriter and the art director. As planners do not write ads themselves, the role of the planning function is to help the people who do, by bringing a consumer perspective to both the development of the overall marketing communications strategy and the creative work.[9]

Here's how one modern planner, Heidi Hackemer, strategic business director at BBH New York, describes her role: "Clarity and inspiration/inspiration and clarity. We have to dig in and find the interesting bits and story and then bring those back to the team so we can collectively create something amazing. We have to constantly make the creative process happen—setting the environments, the bumpers, feeding it and pushing it. We represent the absent in the internal process—planners should be responsible for making sure that the people (the target) and the business are still at the table even when they're physically not."

An insight, says Hackemer, "is the 'why' past the obvious fact. It's the human motivation that precedes the manifested action."

Here's how this planner describes a great copywriter: "A wildly imaginative approach when brainstorming. Someone who understands their own creative idea and where it can and cannot authentically go. Restless with their own solutions. Pushing them. Willing to bin a dead idea and start over, even when they love it—the confidence to know they can come up with something else if needed. A craftsman with words without being a literary bully. Nice."

THE DIGITAL STRATEGIST

Think of the digital strategist as a planner with an acute awareness of everything happening in the digital space—from larger societal trends to the minutiae of data.

The keenly observant may extrapolate from one of the key messages repeated in this book—that digital isn't a channel, it underlies everything now—and wonder if this is a transitional position.

One former digital strategist thinks so. Gareth Kay was a planner at Boston's Modernista! before moving to Goodby Silverstein & Partners and into the role of director of digital strategy. The agency recently appointed him director of brand strategy. Says Kay:

> I think digital strategists are an endangered species. I should know, I was one and I told Derek [Robson, the agency's managing partner] when I joined Goodby that success would be my not having a job in two years. They emerged because strategists lacked digital fluency. This isn't fluency about channel or technology so much as fluency about what digital is doing to culture and human behavior. And because we operate in the category of culture, brands, their communication and the people making them have to change if we are to stay relevant, let alone influence and positively contribute to it.
>
> Digital strategy is much more than a channel. It's about ideas and strategies that are participatory, reciprocal and always on. That evolve over time. That react, not just act. I think digital fluency is a must-have of anyone in advertising, particularly planners. You have to be aware of the culture stuff, and the technology stuff. If you don't, you'll die.
>
> So I think the more interesting question is what is digital doing to strategy and planners. Something I'm trying to figure out now. . . .

MEDIA PLANNER/CHANNEL PLANNER/ COMMUNICATIONS PLANNER

Here's another role that has and will continue to evolve post-internet. A media planner was, one might guess, the expert in which media channels and vehicles would be best used to distribute ad messages. Needless to say, though this is still a function of the media planner, it's a narrow way of looking at the role.

Paul Woolmington, founding partner of Naked Communications, says the media or communications planner of the future will be less about how you manufacture a certain type of communication and more about strategic thinking, solving problems for the client. Like other disciplines, comms planners have fallen into the trap of being too executional.

The perfect comms planner will be multi-dimensional with an understanding of content, context, contact and culture. In other words, you have to understand the channels and that includes understanding sales channels and not just media channels. And you have to understand the content, too, and what content should be served where at what time. In fact, being a great comms planner in the future will be more like being a great creative—knowing what content to produce in what context—the craft skills will exist more at the production level.

I think we'll have media planners who are experts in channels. You're sometimes going to need someone with incredible depth in mobile, or digital, at a level you can't get necessarily from a generalist. So we'll also see planners evolving to operate in teams: maybe one person is the cultural expert, understanding how these things play into people's lives; maybe one person is a content expert, knowing what content works in which channels; and another person might be a data-analytics expert, seeing pictures in the masses of data that we collect today. And we'll need the super-generalists too, to pull all this together.

CREATIVE TECHNOLOGIST

Your resident über-nerd. A creative technologist contributes expertise on what's possible from a technical standpoint and also instigates, bringing awareness of new technologies into creatives' field of vision.

Here's how some of the highest profile creative technologists defined their role in a report in *Creativity*. Dave Cox, technical director at digital agency Lean Mean Fighting Machine: "In its broadest sense my job is to be a facilitator. I do everything I can to never say no to the creatives. There's always a fair amount of nuts and bolts development to be done, and that will always be the case and we can be creative with how to do that well. More than that, though, is being part of the creative process, working through ideas with the creatives to achieve a common goal is where it's at."

Richard Schatzberger, director of creative technology at full-service agency BBH New York: "[My role] really was to be a fusion point of how we bring different perspectives, different opportunities to projects at the right time. I came from a user experience side, but also I have a love for new technologies and new ways of connecting people, new ways people can interact with content—[so I try to] bring those things early into the concept. Every two weeks I give a presentation about the coolest things that have been going on lately—who are all the different players, how do people interact with different things, what are some of the ideas we have been talking about internally that may have not been exposed to the whole agency that brands could benefit from."

AGENCY PRODUCER

The agency producer is the person charged with taking your idea and making it happen. Again, in the TV era this was a more one-dimensional proposition, though by no means a simple one. Agency producers were the experts in directors, in editors, in music. They were the experts in the entire TV spot–production process, from shooting on location to visual effects, as well as being the keepers of the budget and the schedule. Now, as a brand idea can be just about anything, they are experts in . . . everything.

And they are an increasingly integrated part of the creative team. In the digital world, the lines between creation and production have blurred. Particularly in the digital/integrated/idea space, a savvy producer may inform the whole direction of the project by, for example, bringing in tech solutions that add a new dimension or change the nature of an idea.

WHAT ARE AGENCIES LOOKING FOR?

Where do you fit in? What sorts of copywriters will be the best partners for a creative technologist? How do you prepare yourself for this new world of collaboration, and how do you distinguish yourself from a whole universe full of writers?

Each agency and each creative director have their own set of criteria, but among the wish lists of creatives from across the spectrum, some key requirements emerged.

Among them:

Writers who go past big ideas and have a sense of, and interest in, execution.

Writers who are already doing creative things under their own steam. Many creative directors discussed hiring people not based on their ad school portfolio, but on some other creation that they had discovered, something that existed online or somewhere else in the world. If random people are making Super Bowl spots now for shits and giggles, what are you doing?

Collaborators, people who want to share their ideas and work. Also, people who aren't dicks. The era of the preening prima donna creative is over, unfortunately. It was fun for a few people while it lasted. It's more fun for everyone else now.

And, once again, writers who can write.

Close readers will have discerned by now that ideas are important, that copywriters today are thinking beyond traditional ad forms. But ideas aren't enough. There is still writing to be done—as we've demonstrated, great non-ad ideas can often require even more writing than traditional ads, whether that comes in establishing back story and tone, articulating the scope and meaning of the idea for clients, writing scripts, maintaining an ongoing social media presence, writing a brand book or any of a number of other forms of written expression.

Zach Canfield, the director of talent at Goodby Silverstein & Partners, says his challenge is not just finding the people with neat ideas and masters of the one-liner, but finding "writer's writers," the description earned by Goodby's outgoing ECD Steve Simpson.

"Jeff [Goodby] has said a writer's writer is someone who can write more than a couple of sentences in a row," says Canfield. "What I see in a lot of schools, well, they teach writing, which means a lot of headlines. So you know you can see a couple of good sentences but after that it falls off really fast. I never look for just a line. I look for people who are really good at what they do. Sometimes you see people who are too much the generalist. They have to be conceptually strong, but that's only one half; they have to be good writers; they have to be able to write great dialogue; they have to be able to write good scripts. And so if someone comes in and says 'you know I'm conceptually really strong' but they can't really dive deep, I'm going to keep looking."

Most agency creatives and recruiters at forward-leaning agencies are looking for writers who have real skill in writing, but who also have a head for execution, who know or are interested in knowing about how their ideas will become real. This is the challenge for writers today. Agencies are looking for both generalists and experts, in one person, people who have a clear, well-developed skill—in this case writing—but who are also collaborative, tech savvy, and hands on.

"If you can find someone who thinks outside of just the job that we're giving them, so instead of just hiring a writer, you can hire someone who knows what it's like to actually keep an audience captive or what it's like to actually produce something, someone who actually thinks about how it's going to be shot and the best way to edit it as they're writing it, you know those people are golden," says Canfield.

Scott Duchon, ECD at Agencytwofifteen and one of the creators of the award-winning Halo 3 Believe campaign calls these polymaths "five-tool players." "We bring in smart, big-ideas people who can write, and then you expand those skills," says Duchon. "When we bring in other people who have different skill sets we can then take on what they know and apply it to what we do. We talk about it in terms of baseball players—the people who don't only just hit but people who can also run and field, etc.[10] If you can do all five in baseball, there's nothing you can't do. Of course that won't work with everyone, but if you're creating an environment where there are more people who have an understanding of more of the process, it's fulfilling for creatives; they feel like they're learning and growing."

Of course not every player is a five tooler—many creative directors acknowledge that their teams contain those who are exceptionally good at a narrower range of things, and those people can be indispensable. But the important point is about mind-set—the willingness to collaborate, to learn as much as possible about the issues and skills that affect the work beyond writing.

More and more, as the nature of brand creativity evolves, and as brands look for better ways of building stories and having ongoing conversations with consumers, agencies and other creative entities are bringing writers and other creatives from outside the "advertising" world into the brand-creativity world.

COPYWRITER'S TIP

DO STUFF

Perhaps the best tip for copywriters—for anyone, really—that's been dispensed in adland comes from BBH co-founder John Hegarty, who has been known to say, "Do interesting things and interesting things will happen to you." Even if it's not directly "career" related, pursuing creative projects of genuine interest can only lead to good things. It's amazing how often these side projects end up changing people's lives. Create your own version of Google's famed "20 percent time," even if that time has to come from your XBox allotment.

In Goodby's case, this has meant bringing in people from the improv and sketch comedy world, and tapping those who had already found an audience with different content formats online.

Canfield says the agency has cast its recruitment net outside of the ad space and has found writers who have demonstrated competence beyond the headline. "We've done really well with writers who didn't come from advertising backgrounds who are great dialogue writers," says Canfield. "They are used to working for people like *The Daily Show,* where they don't just write one or two sentences and then go show it to their creative director. They're used to writing hundreds of sketches and ideas and skits and intros for people. Those are the type of writers I like—people who can, you know, write for days and don't fall off after the first couple of sentences."

Canfield found one writer when he (the writer) was performing as a rapping donut. "It's not like I went to these comedy shows looking for recruits, but I had been seeing these shows for a few years and I just started to realize, this is kind of like advertising; you have to get in and get out fast you have to be entertaining. He did really well and once that happens it kind of gave us a little more permission to go into those different worlds a little bit and start getting more people like that in the agency. We have a pretty good group of people from different backgrounds now."

Chapin Clark, R/GA SVP managing director, copywriting, says the agency's writers are a "diverse bunch," reflecting the broad range of work that a big digital shop like R/GA is doing. "We have people

THE JOB SEARCH CAN BE PART OF YOUR PORTFOLIO

There are likely few among you who need to be told to "get creative" when it comes to looking for a job.

The bar has been raised a bit here; there have been many, many well-publicized self-promotional gambits, some more worthy of attention than others. Creative directors and others in the hiring role are likely a little burned out by wacky stunts contriving to get their attention. But they never tire of smart, interesting bootstrapped initiatives that demonstrate a proactive nature and a grasp of selling.

The best direct self-marketing efforts show that the author understands how ideas can be created and distributed now and what makes something inspire conversation and sharing.

There have been several high-profile cases of the creative job search gambit being enough to seal the deal.

In May 2010, copywriter Alec Brownstein spent $6 on a Google AdWords scheme to get the attention of prospective employers. When high-profile creative directors David Droga, Ian Reichenthal, Scott Vitrone, Gerry Graf and Tony Granger Googled themselves, the top result was Brownstein's personal message to the creative and a link to his site. Brownstein got four interviews and one job, at Y&R, from the effort, and his YouTube case study video has been viewed nearly a million times.

from film and journalism, from general advertising agencies and digital-centric shops, from graduate advertising programs and from the client side," says Clark. "They're all good at different things. Seldom, if ever, do you find a single person who is great at short-form and long-form writing, at conceptual thinking and the actual craft of writing. Generalists do exist, however, and they are essential to the smooth functioning of an agency—solid writers and thinkers, who have varied subject-matter experience and whom, in a pinch, you can plug in wherever you need them."

AKQA London's Daniel Bonner says,

> We stopped looking for a defined type of creative with the dream CV (you know the one with three or more top agencies on it already and a wealth of "above the line" AND "digital" work and

awards) probably ten or more years ago when it became obvious to us that those people essentially do not exist. Our creatives and writers (they are one and the same, by the way) do not fit one particular mould other than their tenacious ambition to do something different, game changing or just simply better than has ever been done before. A lot of creatives are looking to "get into digital." I'm not entirely sure what that means, but experience has brought us to the conclusion that those creatives are ticking a box or fitting in with a trend they have recognized to be interesting and possibly good for their career. This is not good. We are attracted to creative people who are not happy with the conventions and formulas of the way things are done today (including what exists online and is already "digital" or digitally enabled) and want to invent, innovate and feel a little sick with nervousness because they are not even sure if what they are dreaming of doing can be done.

While many have lamented that the craft of writing has suffered in the internet age, many others believe, in sum, that the kids are all right.

Simpson says writers are now judged less as writers, and more as thinkers, which is, he says a positive development.

I think most people write well, I believe that the internet has made more people writers, and so there are many more good writers among us—and I would argue that the general level of writing has improved or at least not suffered. Writing is a less precious act now, with less obvious models (why would Gossage try to sound so British?), and so there is more originality in the writing I am seeing. It also affected the way we hired new people. Rather than simply recycling talent from other good agencies, as we had in the past, we began to go outside the circle. To academics. To performance artists. And, of course (but to a lesser extent than you might think), to "digital designers." One of my favorite examples is Pete Conolly, who came to us from the UCLA Media Lab, where he'd been teaching. He was hired on the strength of one video he'd created. He'd never worked in advertising before. Within weeks of his hiring, he was instrumental in shaping one of our major campaigns for HP.

There are always areas for improvement among newer writers, though, and they are often acknowledged with a laughing reference to the critic's own curmudgeonly ways. Says R/GA's Clark:

OK, I'm going to channel an angry 80-year-old man for a moment. I find a lot of advertising writers seem to think the actual business of writing—crafting an elegant paragraph, or a blog post that builds and sustains a theme, or whatever—is distasteful. They want to exist purely on this mystical Big Idea plane and either don't care to or don't want to get their hands dirty writing content. For some younger copywriters the concept of paying dues, of learning your craft by cranking out product copy, direct marketing copy, doesn't seem to exist anymore, which is a shame. Because that kind of work makes you better, and doing it well convinces others who are in a position to assign meatier projects to trust you with them. For me, it's a turn-off. I like working with writers who will happily charge into the weeds, who want to learn everything—who are willing to admit they don't know everything—and aren't so precious about what they do.

As several digital creative directors point out, what has emerged as a key writing skill is a flair for dialog. Not the sales pitch or banter of characters in a commercial, but real dialog. If marketing is a conversation, agencies need people who can talk to other people, who can say things that don't sound like ad copy, and who respond when engaged.

Gaston Legorburu, worldwide creative director for digital agency Sapient Nitro, says he looks for "cultural junkie geniuses." "Talent is worth much more than experience in this role," says Legorburu. "We put less emphasis on being able to write a headline, and more value on the ability to write dialogue. A consumer's relationship to a brand is built from a series of interactions. What is not only said, but learned at the first date informs the dialogue on the second, etc. This is an emerging skill. A seasoned adman or journalism student is less likely to grasp and master this than a screen or play writer."

A NEW ROLE FOR A SOCIAL WORLD: BRAND JOURNALISTS

Ad agencies are full of copywriters who came to the profession from journalism—everyone from Leo Burnett to Bill Wright and Greg Hahn were fully or partially formed ink-stained wretches before going to the dark side. Most of the journos who joined the industry pre-2005 ended up honing their craft writing radio, print and TV ads, and then, in many cases, going on to create and contribute to a range of ideas beyond the traditional framework—like Hahn's experience writing short films for BMW and interactive narrative for HBO. Most of the journalists who came to advertising either started out in journalism schools and then switched tracks or worked for a short time in journalism and then made the leap via ad schools.

Today, some of the journalists who are being recruited into the brand world are applying their reporting skills a little more directly.

In 2009, Ty Montague, then CCO of JWT New York formed a ragtag group within the large agency to do what he was calling, for lack of a better term, brand journalism. That phrase wasn't new. It had been coined by, of all people, Larry Light, former CMO of McDonald's.

In an *Ad Age* piece in 2004, Light said that mass marketing was dead and his "brand journalism" concept was "the end of brand positioning as we know it." A brand's marketing, he said, should encompass many stories, not a single one-size-fits-all message. "Any single ad, commercial or promotion is not a summary of our strategy," said Light. "It's not representative of the brand message. . . . We don't need one big execution of a big idea. We need one big idea that can be used in a multidimensional, multi-layered and multifaceted way." To Light, brand journalism was a way to record "what happens to a brand in the world."[11]

Montague created the JWT's brand journalism initiative for client Microsoft, specifically for the tech giant's enterprise business. Dubbed "BIEB" (Because It's Everybody's Business), the effort was a combination of journalism, PR, blogging and social media and advertising and essentially produced an ongoing, up-to-the-minute conversation between Microsoft's marketing and tech people and the IT community that Microsoft targeted with its products. As Montague put it, geeks don't listen to advertising, they listen to other geeks. The BIEB team, including ECD Justin Crawford, Head of Experience Ingrid Bernstein and Kyle Monson, a former *PC Mag* editor and now senior technology editor, monitored the online conversation happening around the relevant products and topics, and when something significant bubbled up from a blog or other source, would draw from a pool of contributors that included hard-core product-development geeks from Microsoft and coordinate a response, often in the form of a blog post. The team would also activate conversations in the form of audio interviews with key geeks, roundtable discussions and other initiatives; ad budgets were devoted to creating hyper-current content around the topics being discussed around the web.

Monson says that in many ways the job overseeing brand journalism at JWT is actually not a huge departure from what he'd been doing on the non–brand journalism side. "I crawl my news feeds and suggest stories for our team of bloggers, write a ton of headlines, edit some of our campaign's written content, and develop broader content and social media strategies for the team to implement. Each day, my team puts a media/conversation monitoring report together for our client, along with recommendations for how we should respond to the stories and conversations that affect our client's products. We might decide to publish a blog post responding to something online, or we'll tweet a URL of favorable media coverage, or we'll traffic a quick-turn-around ad to highlight a great blog post that just went online."

The difference? "The content I produce now has to serve the client's overall messaging goals, at least when taken as a whole," says Monson. "Meaning we can't be too overbearing with our competitive messaging, we want to be transparent, we need to align with PR and marketing goals but without being too 'sell-y.' Those are considerations I never had to make before. The considerations I used to make would deal with things like the potential traffic for a piece of content—I'm still biased in favor of content that's going to make a huge splash, even though that isn't usually as important as meeting campaign goals."

Perhaps more significant is that Monson and those like him, raised outside of the ad world and its assumptions, are bringing into agencies a new perspective on the realities of the marketplace. Monson continues:

> I'm not entirely sure what advertising should be now. I watch lots of TV but almost no commercials, I read lots of magazines but I can't remember a print ad I've seen lately. . . . I don't think I've ever clicked on a banner ad on purpose. . . . I read several corporate blogs, I follow several brands on Twitter, I use Groupon and Yelp and Foursquare, and I try to support and talk about companies that make great products. So brands have plenty of ways to reach me, and I'm more than willing to be an advocate for brands that win me over. If the ad industry thinks I'm the future of media consumption (as I do), then we as an industry are going to have to do better about reaching people like me.

Another writer/journalist and curator, Maria Popova, occupies a unique creative role within TBWA\Chiat\Day. Popova has amassed a large Twitter following as @brainpicker and created and edits the blog

BrainPickings.org, whose mandate is "curating eclectic interestingness from culture's collective brain." She was recruited by Chiat\Day L.A. CCO Rob Schwartz to bring that cultural currency into the agency.

"My job is closely related to what I do in these cultural spaces— offer the agency a stream of curated insights, trends and patterns across the larger cultural context in which brand communication lives," says Popova. "This takes shape as anything from biweekly creative technology workshops . . . to Pirate Pickings, a BrainPickings spinoff on Tumblr offering a curated destination for interestingness across the media arts and creative culture to inform and inspire the agency's work, to consulting on digital strategy and various aspects of consumer psychology (my formal academic background) for different brand teams." In the meantime, Popova continues her work at BrainPickings and continues to write for Wired U.K., *The Huffington Post* and *GOOD Magazine.* "It's part of my own brand, and what helps me stay grounded in the cross-disciplinary contexts that enable me to be a strategic resource at Chiat."

THE CREATIVITY OF CROWDS

In the days after YouTube became a phenomenon, consumer-generated content was all the rage in adland.

The industry's view of the significance and power and opportunity of audience creativity has perhaps gained sophistication.

There are still marketers and campaigns that turn to consumers for ad ideas. The Doritos "Crash the Super Bowl" campaign gives anyone with an idea and a video camera the chance to create the brand's most high-profile ads of the year. The marketer launched the contest in 2007, and in 2009, one of the 1,900 ads submitted for the contest, "Free Doritos," ended up atop *USA Today*'s notorious Ad Meter, which purports to measure the popularity of spots in the game.

Two self-described "nobodies from nowhere," brothers Dave and Joe Herbert, created the ad for a reported $2,000 and won the $1 million in prize money that Frito Lay had promised to anyone who cracked the Ad Meter top three.[12]

The idea behind consumer-generated content, though, is bigger than just sending an open brief out and having aspiring filmmakers create ads.

The term "crowdsourcing" was first used in a 2006 *Wired* article written by Jeff Howe. Here's the money shot from that piece: "Technological advances in everything from product design software to digital video cameras are breaking down the cost barriers that once separated amateurs from professionals. Hobbyists, part-timers, and dabblers suddenly have a market for their efforts, as smart companies in industries as disparate as pharmaceuticals and television discover ways to tap the latent talent of the crowd. The labor isn't always free, but it costs a lot less than paying traditional employees. It's not outsourcing; it's crowdsourcing."[13]

It's still a useful way to sum up the changes that have been remaking industries like advertising and journalism and nearly everything else besides surgery.

In recent years, some industry players have looked to create business models to harness the abundance of creativity.

In 2009, John Winsor, who had most recently been VP/executive director of strategy and innovation at Crispin Porter + Bogusky, lit out to start his own agency, Victors & Spoils. Winsor had a background in journalism; prior to joining CP+B he had founded a magazine-publishing business focusing on sports titles.

He partnered with CP+B creative director Evan Fry and Claudia Batten, a co-founder of video game ad serving company Massive, to create what he called the first ad agency built on crowdsourcing principles. The company would have the same core strategic and management and creative direction leadership as a typical agency, but instead of maintaining a large, full-time creative department, the partners would use, theoretically, every creative person on the internet. The shop used both existing crowdsource-based creative services like Crowdspring and its own custom-built database of creatives.

"If you're a mid-level person, an art director or copywriter, creativity has become a commodity," says Winsor. "In a world of scarcity, a few people have the right technology, the right training to do a job. What works well in that scenario is command and control, organizations that charge a fee for access to those assets. We're in a world of abundance; everyone has the same tools, the same ability to tell stories. And we're not geographically constrained anymore; people can work from all over the globe. You can't fight the trend of democratization."

As for the lamentation about the loss of craft, Winsor says it's "like the Louis XV court complaining that the common people were getting the vote. It's a paradigm shift. The notion of this is our craft, we own it, to me as an outsider, it's a historic artifact. There's still craft to it but the craft comes in creative direction."

But surely Winsor has been on YouTube; there's a lot of creativity out there, but there's also a lot of other stuff to which one would be hard-pressed to ascribe any merit, creative or otherwise.

Winsor cites Sturgeon's Law, an elegant, universally applicable declaration that "90 percent of everything is crud."

"90 percent is crap, 9 percent is good and 1 percent is great," says Winsor. "That's the same dynamic as in agencies."

Predictably, most of the people who ended up satisfying the early V&S briefs tended to be creatives working at other agencies. But Winsor says there are others—journalists and other kinds of writers starting to get into the act. "Writing TV scripts and certain kinds of copy, they are very specific so there is a big learning curve. But my sense is that with all these platforms and things opening up, new people can get involved and play and be trained and learn to do it pretty quickly."

There is a simple supply-and-demand equation, says Winsor, that will put downward pressure on high-paying agency jobs. "The same thing happened in journalism. In 2004 when I started blogging, all my journalist friends said that's so stupid, this whole blogging thing will never last, nothing will substitute for our journalistic integrity." Winsor likens big agencies to the movie studios of yore that owned all the talent in the filmmaking process. "I bet you could find studio people back then saying, oh, you could never make a movie any other way."

Adam Glickman, co-founder and former editor of *Tokion* magazine and creative partner at BBH New York, launched his own crowd-sourced creativity platform, The IdeaLists, in 2010. The IdeaLists is an open-source creative agency/matchmaking service. It allows creatives to post their great ideas in hopes of finding a backer or partner to realize them and also allows individuals and companies—brands, bands, media outlets, whoever—to post briefs and find creative talent to work with (The IdeaLists was used to find the designer of this book's cover).

"There's a new business model where there are bigger rewards for the sharing of info rather than the controlling of info," says Glickman. "I'm proposing that the best idea might come from outside of your company."

Traditional agencies are challenged, he says, on a couple of fronts. First, though they get a bad rap for not being experimental enough, they can only move as quickly as their clients; "they're not allowed to think two or three years down the road, they can only think six months down the road." And agencies, says Glickman, have a "big idea" legacy that makes it harder for them to come up with the kind of smaller, ongoing ideas that work in today's media landscape. "Agencies are built on the 'big idea,' what's one big idea around which they can create a broad and shallow campaign that can speak to a lot of people. Nowadays it seems more and more that clients need multiple smaller, deeper and narrower executions. Clients may say, I don't need a single million-dollar solution, I need a hundred ten-thousand-dollar executions. That's what I'm tooling IdeaLists to do."

THE FUN FACTOR

Were there more "characters" back in the days when you could smoke in your office? Maybe. There is a degree to which some of the "fun" has been sucked out of the industry. Periods of economic hardship have been known to take their toll on excessive gaiety.

Every company is working harder, doing more with fewer people. In most companies, there isn't a lot of time for standing around. But, for most creatives, fun is in creating. And on that score, there has never been a more rewarding time.

Are there fewer boozy lunches and coke-fuelled Christmas parties now? Yes to the former (though the latter seems to be undergoing something of a resurgence). Ideally, you'll have a Brit or other European on your team. They will take the lead on ordering alcohol at lunch so you'll feel more comfortable joining in, if that's something you're interested in.

But here's something to remember: there was a downside to all that "fun" people (men) were having back in the day. Some of those "characters" were also sometimes those men who literally or figuratively chased their "girl" around the desk. They were sometimes those men whose bullying and anger issues were passed off as "intensity."

All the vices are still there—more of them are just kept out of the workplace.

And if you ever doubt that philandering has gone out of the industry, a quick trip to Cannes will relieve you of that delusion.

A WORD ABOUT AWARDS

Speaking of Cannes, if you wind up at a decent agency, you'll likely get some sort of award over the course of your career.

Awards are nice. For agencies, they act as a recruitment tool— more creatives want to work for the agency that's known for doing good work, and one of the primary measures of an agency's creative standards has been the number of trophies flung around its office, so the cycle continues. Some agency execs insist that clients care about awards, too, so Cannes Lions and One Show Pencils act as a new business tool. And there have certainly been more clients going to Cannes these days.

But, like many things the ad industry once thought were important, ad awards are tending to lose their luster.

If you're writing for awards judges, you're in it for all the wrong reasons. It'd be nice to say if you're writing for awards judges, you won't have a long career. But it's not entirely clear that that's true. Awards are still given to suspect entries—those ads that run once at 4 A.M. on the local station in Bend, Oregon. There are marketers who create slush funds to back work that's specifically intended to win awards, and then go back to doing crappy work for the rest of the year. So it turns out that there are some people who have done quite well from creating work to win awards.

But awards centrism seems more and more anachronistic.

There are so many more significant ways now to measure how successful, how "creative" your work is. Focus on the important things—how well your idea works for the brand, and for the audience. If you do that, awards will likely come too.

And when you do go to Cannes, you are encouraged to get horribly drunk and behave badly.

THAT'S GREAT, BUT WHAT'S IT REALLY LIKE?

A few copywriters take us through their day . . .

24 HOURS WITH JORDAN CHOUTEAU,
JUNIOR COPYWRITER, MOTHER NEW YORK

6:15 A.M.	Alarm one. Turn off. Go back to bed.
7:15 A.M.	Alarm two. Turn off. Get up.
7:20 A.M.	Head out door to clock five or seven miles. Which depends on how late I was at work the night before and/or if I'm hung over.
8:30 A.M.	Take shower. Get dressed.
9:00 A.M.	Walk ten minutes to Mother.
9:10 A.M.	Arrive at Mother. Doctor up a cup of coffee. Pour a bowl of Cheerios. Eat and drink both.
9:30 A.M.	Check emails. Check Facebook. Check my go-to bookmarks.
10:00 A.M.	Time to start the day. And at Mother there is no such thing as a typical day. But there is such a thing as a typical process. It starts when we are handed a brief. Our days are then spent "concepting," a term creatives use for brainstorming. These are the days my partner April Mathis (who is awesome, FYI) and I lay claim to the very few, very popular couches around Mother or head out to find a quiet café or a dark hotel lobby. The Smile typically wins.

There we think, talk, think, stare at one another, break to gossip about a dude, order a coffee, complain about the brief, stumble upon an idea, build on that idea, decide we hate that idea, kill that idea, come up with another idea, then another idea, decide we have two good ideas, then decide we deserve a break.

After a few days of that, we present our magic making to our creative director. He (I've yet to have a she) oohs, ahhs, smiles, questions, kills, points and usually picks one, maybe two, maybe five ideas. The next few days are spent repeating that whole think, talk, stare process to explore the ideas further. And then it happens. It all becomes clear and we "nail it." It's that time we know we've got something. Something good.

Then it's GO TIME. We hit our respective Macs. April art directs. I write. And write. And write some more. Until finally, we've got a PDF filled with work backed by Paul, Linus, and the rest of the gang, ready for client.

Present to client.

Wait for feedback.

Get feedback.

Repeat . . .

2:00 P.M.	Lunch. Usually a salad. Always with goat cheese.
2:30 P.M.	Repeat 10:00 A.M.–2:00 P.M. But this time harder. Why? Because maybe, just maybe, there's a chance I can catch that 8 o'clock yoga class or I can go on that date, with that dude that I've rescheduled on three times too many . . .
8:00 P.M.	Texting that dude to reschedule for Friday, maybe Sunday.
11:00 P.M.	Sitting at my desk writing headlines. Uncomfortable from all the sushi I just crushed. The sushi I'll expense three months from now . . . if I get some time.
1:00 A.M.	Screw this. I'm going home.

24 HOURS WITH LEA PLATZ, COPYWRITER, KIRSHENBAUM BOND SENECAL & PARTNERS

7:30 A.M.	Snooze.
7:39 A.M.	Snooze.

7:48 A.M.   Snooze.

7:57 A.M.   Rush.

9:20 A.M.   Arrive at office; see my partner has arrived before me.

9:23 A.M.   Retreat to kitchen. Parisian Nights? Or Rainforest Espresso?

9:25 A.M.   Field generic weekend inquiries. Reciprocate.

9:28 A.M.   Return to desk. Organize ideas from the night before for a skincare line that admits that as it stands, it stands for nothing.

9:35 A.M.   Channel my inner 25-year-old girl who is experiencing the best skin of her life, but has no concept she is currently experiencing the best skin of her life. Notice a zit.

9:36 A.M.   Begin writing.

10:00 A.M.   Creative department starts to populate. Put on headphones, leave music off. Create invisible psychic barrier in open-style office.

10:45 A.M.   Relish the fact that we're not checking boxes here. It's not what's the mandatory print/TV/digital/outdoor execution—it's no holds barred, get quarter-life crisis chick's attention.

11:00 A.M.   Fantasize about re-launching the brand totally gesture-based so none of it can be ASI tested.

12:30 P.M.   Scan office for any client- or rep-lunch leftovers in the building. No luck. Return to desk.

1:15 P.M.   Notice figure hovering respectfully in peripheral vision. And wait for it, wait for it . . .

1:16 P.M.   Shoulder tap. Remove headphones. Discuss timings with project manager.

2:13 P.M.   Take typed-up concepts to partner.

2:20 P.M.   Puzzlement as to why art directors are always better spellers.

2:43 P.M.	Brief "Yeah, but is that using Twitter just to use Twitter? Or do we think that's actually a good idea?" conversation.
3:03 P.M.	Google our favorite tagline, cross fingers it didn't seep into our brains from the collective advertising unconscious and is already out there.
3:10 P.M.	It's not.
3:45–3:59 P.M.	Mutual ego-stroking.
4:00 P.M.	Present to creative director. Scan body language cues. What is she liking . . .
4:42 P.M.	Three directions move forward. Start revising work for account meeting tomorrow.
6:45 P.M.	Direction #3 is rapidly losing its pulse. It has become obvious it shares vital organs with direction #2.
7:39 P.M.	Direction #3 time of death
8:11 P.M.	Coming up with more bad puns than good headlines.
8:23 P.M.	Order Thai. Eat too much.
8:45 P.M.	Look for inspiration online.
8:50 P.M.	Inspiration and entertainment blur.
9:00 P.M.	Hey, how long do you want to stay tonight? I dunno, how long do you want to stay? I could go soon. Do you want to go? I could work from home . . .
9:10 P.M.	Hail cab.
9:23 P.M.	Walk into apartment. Sigh. You're trying to tell me something, aren't you?
9:25 P.M.	Clean up Cujo-shredded wee-wee pad.
9:31 P.M.	Wagging tail.
9:45 P.M.	Zero desire to work at home.

10:46 P.M.	"In the criminal justice system, sexually based offenses are considered especially heinous . . ."
12:10 A.M.	Should have written more headlines.
12:13 A.M.	Guilt.
12:17 A.M.	Anxiety.
12:24 A.M.	Bargaining.
12:27 A.M.	I'll just get up early.

24 HOURS WITH CHAPIN CLARK, SVP, MANAGING DIRECTOR, COPYWRITING, R/GA

Most mornings on my commute into work I'm scanning Twitter and my Google Reader feeds to see what's going on and if there's anything worth tweeting for @RGA. For me, the need to tweet is reflexive. It's involuntary, like breathing or swallowing food. Sad, but true. Regardless, I like to have something out there by 9 or 9:30 A.M.

On an average day, much of my time is given over to—surprise!—meetings. As head of copy, I do a lot of managerial work—recruiting-related things like portfolio reviews and interviews, sorting out staffing issues, strategizing how we want to build out our new offices in São Paulo, Buenos Aires, and Singapore. I'm looking at portfolios and interviewing candidates pretty much constantly.

This morning I met with a junior copywriter candidate for our Verizon team. He has an unconventional background—including four years in the Army's First Infantry Division and a current gig as a security guard at an office building downtown—but a fantastic attitude and a portfolio with some good thinking in it. He is young but has seen the world, so he's seasoned and has a broader perspective than most people his age. Also uncharacteristic for his peer group: not a shred of entitlement. I think he's going to be a great fit for our Verizon team—and ecstatic to get the job offer.

Giving a junior person the opportunity to do more, to stretch and take on more responsibility, and making someone genuinely happy, at once—it doesn't get better than that.

I'm usually involved with one or two clients at any given time. Right now I'm focused on a large financial services client and our impending redesign of their public website. The last couple of weeks I've been spending a lot of time at their offices gathering feedback from different business units on what they want to see happen with the new site.

My office is in a very visible, high-traffic location, so I get a lot of drive-by visits from writers and others who want to talk through projects, or vent the frustration they're experiencing with projects. I do a lot of listening, and I try to help however I can—either directly or by pulling in a resource I know can do a better job than I can.

That's how I got involved in a script-doctoring effort for a project we're pitching to one of our consumer packaged goods clients. We're producing a video to help sell the idea, and the script, due to forces beyond any one person's control, had become a bit too long and unfocused. I worked with her and the creative director to tighten it up. Sometimes a pair of fresh eyes, and minimal knowledge of the client's preferences and prejudices, are the best advantage you can have.

Throughout the day, in spare moments or during lunch, I'm checking Twitter and the rest of the web—news sites; business, advertising, and tech blogs; weird personal sites, whatever—as well as what our own writers, designers, and programmers are saying via internal email strings, for something interesting to broadcast. Or I just spend a little time responding to some of my favorite tweeters—usually industry people. As I say, it has become involuntary."

CHAPTER 7

BRINGING IDEAS TO LIFE

We've been referring to this era in advertising as the era of consumer control and to the TV era in the past tense, to convey the enormity of the internet's impact on marketing.

TV is, of course, very much with us. And so is print (for now). And so are outdoor billboards. And so are Twitter feeds, blogs, apps, games and events.

All of these things are the province of the copywriter. It's just that now, no single one of them is the default answer when the writer faces a marketing challenge.

Writers, and everyone involved in the creative process, have the opportunity and the mandate to think in ideas first.

Some creatives, especially digital creatives, are loath to use the expression "big idea." The world is full of too many big ideas, they'd say. Sometimes, as The IdeaLists' Adam Glickman noted, a small idea is best.

In fact, many creatives and pundits now decry the idea, period, citing the crucial importance of execution.

There are valid points here, though for our purposes, they're a little overwrought.

The backlash against the big idea came from the baggage attached to advertising's idea of a big idea. A big idea is often too attached to the notion of a big, overblown advertising idea—a big, overarching message that must say everything to everyone about a brand, that takes a long time and a lot of money to create and that is broadcast out to a specified audience for a finite period of time. A big idea can also conjure up the idea of the Big Integrated Campaign in which, just because you can, you do the TV spots, the micro site, the mobile app, the Facebook page, the Twitter feed and the flash mob.

A big idea is also "Just Do It," which was expressed in everything from TV commercials to Nike+, the iPod-compatible device that tracks running data, to Run London, an initiative to encourage people to sign up for 10K races.

Continue to seek the big idea. But remember that a big idea doesn't have to mean a big campaign. Ideas can and often should be iterative, evolving, interactive and nimble.

So, how do you arrive at the big idea? Or any idea? How do you do something that earns attention and interaction? How do you join people's conversations instead of just shouting messages? And how do you ensure that you're a welcome addition to the conversation? What is a really integrated idea, and what's just matching luggage? What can you make that's useful, beautiful, entertaining or all of those things?

All of these questions and more have been answered by the creatives who wrote and developed some of the most interesting and successful work in the last several years.

In this chapter they talk about their ideas, big and small, and how they turned those ideas into brand content and experiences.

There's insight into how to do a great TV spot, how to create something useful, how to think differently about tag lines, how and when to use print and outdoor. But the point is, you shouldn't necessarily be thinking in any specific medium when you set out to crack a brief.

BRANDED CONTENT BEYOND BMW FILMS:
AXE GAMEKILLERS

In the years since BMW Films, countless marketers and agencies have experimented with new ways to meld brand messages with longer-form entertainment content. With the spread of broadband to more U.S. homes, the barriers to creating satisfying video experiences fell, leaving the remaining more important concern—making something that anyone would want to watch.

At the same time, the advertising world re-established its ties with the TV and feature-film world, with Hollywood. In 2003, *Advertising Age* launched a new content channel and event called "Madison and Vine" to chronicle the action. And there was lots of action.

In 2006, BBH New York created an initiative for Unilever's Axe that upped the ante on branded content. The Unilever brand, known first as Lynx in Europe, was by this time famous for its trademark "friend to the horny man" ad formula. For several years, the brand's ads focused relentlessly on the idea of ordinary guys in the 18–24 demographic getting extraordinarily lucky with any number of uncommonly hot ladies, assisted by an application of apparently irresistible Axe body spray. The campaign originated at BBH London, and the New York agency contributed its fair share to the Axe oeuvre.

When it came time for Unilever to launch a new Axe product, a solid deodorant, BBH turned what was originally a TV campaign idea into a rather groundbreaking branded content initiative. The idea was "Gamekillers," an assortment of characters—like Man With Dog, British Accent Guy, Mother Hen and Sensitivo—who existed only to get between an Axe man and his potential conquest.

The agency team, led by CCO Kevin Roddy and Group Creative Director William Gelner, took the core idea and turned it into a one-hour show that aired on MTV in early 2006. The show followed an average dude as he went on a series of dates while trying to avoid the nookie-nixing intrusions of the Gamekillers. The following year, the show was turned into a full reality series.

The project marked a milestone in the brand/entertainment continuum. It was, and remains, one of the few brand-backed properties to air on TV. It was a marketing idea that turned into a pure entertainment play—the show was not overtly branded and was conspicuously free of any Axe Dry deodorant. The agency created a brand bridge with the look and feel of the show's titles and with interstitial content and commercial, print and web tie-ins. It also marked the new style of collaboration between agencies, production companies and media outlets. BBH brought on @radical.media, which was by this time versed in entertainment production and helped the agency turn its idea into long-form content and helped it maneuver the entertainment landscape.

Roddy, an oft-awarded copywriter, has, as a creative director, leaned into the changes that have been remaking the business of brand creativity. Early in his tenure, he issued a challenge to the BBH creative department that has resulted in a number of significant be-yond-ad measures, including the more recent Oasis *Dig Out Your Soul* campaign.

KEVIN RODDY ON THE CREATION OF "GAMEKILLERS"

In my first couple of weeks at BBH, I took the creative department aside and said that I wanted to expand the definition of "advertising" today. New forms of advertising were emerging, as well as new media, and I wanted to be sure BBH was at the front of that wave and didn't get caught behind it needing to catch up. I also knew that the best way to get people to truly understand what I meant by that was to show them some examples. It's easy to say what you want, but it's eas-ier to inspire agency creative people with great work that points them more clearly in the direction you want them to go. So I was constantly looking for relevant opportunities to try new things.

Interestingly, a few months later on this assignment, a few 30-second TV scripts came across my desk. The idea of gamekillers was in there, but the form was traditional TV spots. That's when I spoke with William Gelner and we decided that the idea could, if we wanted it to, be bigger than just TV commercials. So we threw the TV com-mercial scripts in the trash and started with the idea—in the mating game there are people out to kill your game and this puts incredible pressure on you. But the dryer you can stay, the better your chances of not offending a girl and turning her off.

We decided to think big and not think in terms of "advertising," at least not advertising as we commonly knew it. Which is how we came to the idea of a TV show, and everything stemmed from there.

For me this was important because it was an approach to an as-signment that wasn't linear. The beginnings were the same—there was a traditional advertising brief—but the result was different. I tell people it's not "branded content" (which, to me, implies that the con-tent existed and then we came in to brand it) but, rather, "brand con-tent." Because this was content created specifically by a brand, to an advertising brief.

And then there's another reason I wanted to do this—because Axe is a brand, and an idea, that isn't about "saying," it's about "doing." Axe is an aid in the mating game. It's a tool for guys. And we need to be sure that we behave as a brand, not simply make claims. This was a chance for us to do that.

I think it was an early example of what is far more commonplace today—collaboration. On every level and in every way. Once the idea was out in the open, we broke down the walls of ownership and began involving a lot more people in developing it and expanding it. From the outset we knew that the idea itself didn't have boundaries. It wasn't an advertising idea, it was a truth. And we knew that trying to "control" it the way we can control an ad was only going to punish it. We had to invite people into the idea. Not just in executing it, but in developing it. The characters, the media, everything needed new kinds of people who could help us think in new kinds of ways. And that combination and collaboration was what made everything better.

On Getting Content Right

I honestly think you need to start with a relevant and engaging idea. It can't be an "advertising idea," it needs to be a consumer idea. "Axe helps guys meet girls" . . . that is an idea based around a consumer. It's not something the brand is pushing on consumers about itself, it's an idea about how they can help consumers in something consumers find relevant and appealing. If you have an idea like that as a starting point, you're a long way ahead.

TRANSCENDING CATEGORY NORMS:
MILLER HIGH LIFE, "THE HIGH LIFE MAN"

Well. Old Paul Bunyan must be spinning in his pine box. When a man takes to warming his bones with a counterfeit fire, how far away can he be from succumbing to electric razors, leaf blowers, pleated pants?

America, is that really you?

We've been talking about it for years—the demise, the redundancy, the purposelessness, the existential predicament, the impotent anger of the once dominant gender. In June 2010, *The Atlantic* made it official, with a subtly titled cover story, "The End of Men."

Reports of the death of men, however, have been greatly exaggerated. Men are still very much with us, and a quick glance at the ranks of CEOs, presidents, senators, law firm partners, surgeons, web entrepreneurs—and creative directors—indicates that they're still finding things to do with themselves.

By now it's become something of an advertising standby: exploit the notion of beleaguered masculinity, assume the position of man's best brand friend, helping the stronger sex stay strong.

In most cases, when a brand has gone to the "bring back real men/don't let the bitches grind you down" well, the resulting ads have been forgettable, or just awful—sad for men and annoying for women.

But it wasn't always so.

There was a time when men were celebrated in ads, when unapologetic, unfettered, ungroomed masculinity was saluted with grit, humor, near poignancy.

It was Miller Time.

Wieden+Kennedy Portland's Miller High Life campaign of 1998 to 2004 was an original, enduring moment in beer advertising. The campaign sidestepped the cultural markers of manhood as typically appropriated by brewers—edgy or nostalgic music, disproportionately attractive females, broad, easily relatable humor—and reclaimed masculinity with quiet and disquieting observations about the essence of the American male.

Miller High Life, created in 1903, is Miller's oldest brand. But by the early 1990s, Miller's once proud "Champagne of Beers" had lost its sparkle. A decade of yuppies and the light beers they loved had taken its toll on MHL sales; Miller had stopped advertising the brand and started discounting the price of the beer, putting it in the dreaded "sub-premium" category.

In 1998 with agency partner Wieden, the brewer decided to give the brand another go. It redesigned the MHL label to exploit the beer's heritage and started running a deeply unusual ad campaign.

The Miller High Life ads featured a small slice of everyday life, as observed by the uncompromisingly masculine "High Life Man." In each case, the High Life Man, voiced by Doug Jeffers, would celebrate some simple symbol of life lived as it should be—duct tape, butter-slathered burgers, hot dogs—or bear witness to that life being debased by something that no real man could countenance—fake fireplace logs, the inability to maneuver one's boat trailer, fruit. Nothing much happened in the ads; the camera lingered on frying bacon or a battered garage fridge or the back of a man standing on his lawn and looking disapprovingly at some violation of the male code happening across the street. The men (always men; two of the ads featured women—one a lecturing mother-in-law, the other an eager-to-please new bride buying beer) were working-class types well north of the usual beer demographic. The film looked a little weathered—not archival grainy, but just muted enough to have the vague feel of another time.

The campaign was created by Wieden copywriter Jeff Kling and art director Jeff Williams under creative director and legendary writer Jim Riswold and was directed by acclaimed documentarian Errol Morris.

The ads managed to reclaim the High Life heritage without wallowing in "cool" retro style or nostalgia, but they also appealed to a new generation of beer drinkers who sniffed at advertising that tried too hard to speak their language.

Without resorting to chill irony in the spots themselves, the Miller creatives achieved the remarkable—they allowed the irony to come after the fact—that irony being that younger drinkers loved the archly old school Miller High Life man better than any wannabe hipster peddling manufactured cool.

Kling is respected by many a creative today as a writer's writer. He is also a copywriter who belongs to the let-the-subconscious-do-the-work school. "The answer to almost anything comes to me when I'm doing something different," says Kling. "I know that I have to let my subconscious work on stuff, I have to fuck around; I will get my version of an answer when I'm doing something totally different."

The campaign idea came from that subconscious stew, from the straight-ahead mission to sell beer and save the brand, and from some great account planners.

JEFF KLING ON CREATING THE MILLER HIGH LIFE CAMPAIGN

The brief was so wide open, it was basically just "do something." At this point, the beer was an also-ran, something they maintained because some beer drinkers liked it. But it was tough for them to make money once they started discounting it; a lot of brewers really discounted beers out of existence—once they start doing that, they can't make money on it. Then they have to bring out new products and spend a lot of money to market those. That's why so many beautiful old brands go the way of old things.

In the case of High Life, I was writing a bullshit email to a friend back on the East Coast. Something happened and I thought, Hold on . . . and I opened a new window and started typing thoughts.

Those thoughts formed the basis of what became the "High Life Manifesto," which stated: "only a large-scale decline in American manhood can account for the near disappearance of Miller High Life Beer."

Our thesis on High Life was simple: we knew the beer was in trouble and we needed to sell more. We thought well, man, this beer wouldn't be in trouble if there were any men left to drink it; if this country knew what it meant to be a man anymore, this stuff would be selling and selling and selling. So that's easy. But from there you can get it tonally wrong. And here we had some good planner help. Our planners went out and got some verbatims. Until they did, we were in a sort of smart-alecky, ironic adland sort of voice with the stuff. There were three planners working on it; Claire Grossman was the lead planner, she was a brilliant woman and she brought in two other women, Jen Patterson and Jen Coleman. They went around a few big Midwestern cities talking to guys, and what we briefly outlined was a male profile. It was a real guy, a guy who builds stuff. Those guys said things like "we have no sympathy for the guys in collared shirts who get in their Lexuses at the end of the day and go home and cry into their beer." They were looking down their noses at yuppie culture. Hearing from them in their own voices we knew there was no ad-y jokey bullshit that would make these guys give a shit. Because we had the verbatims we were able to make the people we needed to reach real. Before the verbatims we were also reading the ads as dialog— like a guy behind a counter talking to another guy. Afterwards it seemed like we just wanted to shine a spotlight on a world that was disappearing, a way of thinking that was disappearing. We wanted to force people to look uncomfortably long at something and understand what they were seeing. We wanted to share a sense of humor and importance about a way that was disappearing.

On Execution and Errol Morris

I was blown away by what we saw in Errol's film [*Fast Cheap and Out of Control*, Morris's 1997 documentary]. His camera and his eye would linger on these details that other people would miss. There was one shot—it was an overcranked shot of a topiary gardener. The action is slowed down to this sun-drenched, hypnotic beauty as this guy is trimming a hedge. And we're just looking at the guy rhythmically squeezing the handle on the hedge clipper and without breaking stride he takes his right hand off the handle and ushers this bee that was in the way out of his way and he keeps going. It's the most beautiful detail. The guy had never done anything commercial but we wanted to work with him.

On Believing in Your Idea

We didn't know we were right. You don't know whether you're right. It mostly just works because you can't be afraid to be wrong. That's super important for helping creatives get to things they think are the answer. They have to know that it's OK to be wrong, but they have to believe in the idea. If they believe in it and it moves them, it's going to move other people. As long as it's done in the spirit of generosity and it's heartfelt. If it's snide or smart-alecky or trying to be clever, if it's selfish work, that's going to show up, and it's going to be no fun and it's going to die.

TRANSCENDING CATEGORY NORMS II: DOS EQUIS, "THE MOST INTERESTING MAN IN THE WORLD"

He lives vicariously through himself.

While Kling wrote one of the beer category's greatest campaigns, he was the creative director of (and wrote the signature signoff for) another.

While at Euro RSCG New York in 2007, Kling worked with Karl Lieberman and Brandon Henderson, a creative team that, after several false starts and frustrating go-rounds with layers of clients, conjured a cultural icon—The Most Interesting Man in the World.

The campaign put a lesser-known import in the middle of popular consciousness with a weathered spokesman whose thoroughgoing interestingness made James Bond look like a wallflower. The Most Interesting Man in the World "once had an awkward moment, just to see how it feels"; "people hang on his every word, even the prepositions"; and "the police often question him just because they find him interesting."

The team also created perhaps the only beer campaign in history that features a main character who admits, nearly boasts, "I don't always drink beer."

And what do you know? That didn't dissuade beer drinkers; *Ad Age* reported that through June 2009, a period when imported beer sales dropped 11 percent, sales of Dos Equis rose more than 17 percent.

"There's never really been an import brand that's been built so clearly through advertising," Benj Steinman, publisher of *Beer Marketer's Insights* told *Ad Age*.[1]

Kling says that the agency essentially had two client groups on the brand, the Mexican brewery that brews the beer, Cuauhtémoc Moctezuma and Heineken, which owns and distributes the brand in North America.

"After a lot of hard work and missteps we arrived at the insight that guys more than anything don't want to be thought of as being uninteresting; their biggest fear especially when they go out at night is being the boring guy," says Kling. "So the challenge was, how do you create something that people will pay a little more for? Karl Lieberman and Brian Henderson had the idea for the campaign, 'The Most Interesting Man in the World.' It ran right at the problem."

KARL LIEBERMAN AND BRANDON HENDERSON
TAKE IT FROM THERE

Karl Lieberman: As I remember, the brief was based on some insight around how our target was constantly looking for opportunities to make less-mainstream, more-interesting choices in life. And that, when it came to our target's choice of beer, there was a very large opportunity to capitalize on this phenomenon.

Heineken had acquired the distribution rights to Dos Equis in America and had this notion that Dos Equis could work within their premium portfolio of beers like Amstel and Heineken. We thought it was a pretty bizarre decision at the time, since in our minds, Dos

Equis was pretty much a chaser for chimichangas and chalupas, but in hindsight, they were spot on.

The campaign took a few months to fully bake, so it was influenced by a myriad of things. But it started with just a dead-simple manifesto that, funny enough, eventually became the campaign's first radio spot.

At first, the whole thing was haphazardly thrown together.

About an hour before a mandatory department-wide Dos Equis creative review, we had nothing. This was mostly because a few weeks prior, a Dos Equis campaign we had created called "Say Sí to the Mexican Way" had been pulled from pre-production and killed. So we weren't real hot to work on it again and had instead been focusing our efforts on complaining about stuff and playing XBox.

But, given that we were both terrified of our executive creative director, Jeff Kling, we figured we should try to come up with something for the meeting, even if it was half-baked and awful.

There was a really funny animated rap parody video about George Washington going around the internet at the time that claimed our first president did things like ride atop "a horse made of crystal" and "killed his sensei in a duel and he never said why."[2] It was hilarious. We loved the lore of it. Applying hyperbole to such a historic figure was an awesome idea.

Because we were one of those cliché young and cynical spoiled creative teams, we were highly dubious of this brief that was written around this notion of "interesting." In hindsight, Caroline Wellman and Mary Perhach had put together an excellent strategy, but at the time, we were asking things like, "How could drinking this beer from Mexico make a man seem more interesting?"

Sure, Dos Equis was kind of interesting compared to a twelve-ounce can of light domestic beer, but it wasn't like drinking molten lava or the blood of a rare deep-sea Merman. The whole notion seemed like advertising at its worst to us.

So, we did what all good young obnoxious creatives do: we made fun of the brief.

We decided it would be fun to apply an insane level of hyperbole to someone who is just moderately interesting. If simply drinking Dos Equis purportedly defined this man as a more interesting man, then what else did? We started thinking about the mundane things we hated about ourselves and then had The Most Interesting Man In The World do the opposite.

It was the whole "write what you know" angle, but what we did was write the opposite of what we knew. This netted language like:

"He's never once alphabetized his DVD collection."

"He doesn't get his salad dressing on the side of the salad, he gets it on top of the salad. Where it belongs."

Over the next couple of months, we worked on the language around the man's lore and tried to figure out what he himself would be like.

Given that it takes a lifetime to acquire this much experience, we always imagined him as an older gentleman. We referenced guys like Sean Connery's James Bond, Ben Gazzara's Jackie Treehorn character in *The Big Lebowski* and David Carradine in *Kill Bill*. To give a nod to the beer's heritage, we made him Latino. We also figured he should have a beard, since neither Brandon nor I had the ability to grow facial hair. And I'm pretty sure the unbuttoned, disheveled tuxedo was inspired by an excellent photo we had of Wayne Newton sitting in a bar with some Vegas showgirls.

We figured Dos Equis should feature The Most Interesting Man in its advertising the way Nike featured Michael Jordan. While Jordan was without question the world's greatest basketball player, we thought it was funny for Dos Equis to have the same confidence and the audacity to declare this gentleman "The Most Interesting Man In The World."

With all those things seeming to work together, the last piece of copywriting we had to figure out was how the man would speak. What would he say if given the opportunity? Jeff Kling's direction was that he needed to speak in a way that was both his voice and the voice of Dos Equis. The Most Interesting Man In The World needed to have a "more interesting" take on the world—an "enlightened" one, albeit mostly about beer.

That led us to the guiding principle of his voice: WWBD?—What Wouldn't Budweiser Do? After that, the language of that part of the campaign came relatively easily:

"Happy hour is the hour after happy hour is over."

"Find out what it is in life that you don't do well. And then don't do that thing."

We'd look at what we considered meat-headed, lowest-common-denominator thinking and try to flip it on its head.

I can't remember the specifics, but I think this whole process of getting from a manifesto to a full campaign with TV and print and whatnot took a couple of months. There were a bunch of other excellent campaigns in the mix during this time, but somehow, round after round, The Most Interesting Man kept surviving. Even through testing. Which was amazing. Because at one point, we actually tested whether or not he should have a beard. (The beard tested well.)

Brandon Henderson: The only thing I'd add is an observation about our original idea for Dos Equis, "Say Sí to the Mexican Way." That idea was based on a pretty boring strategy, which was, "The Authentic Mexican Beer." It was un-insightful, and the work reflected it.

After that campaign died, the planner came back with the new insight that young men's biggest fear was that they were uninteresting. That did strike us as insanely true. That's why people lie about their job titles. That's why people embellish stories. That's why, before he went to the moon, Edwin Aldrin changed his name to Buzz. With an insight like that, it was much easier to do good work.

Karl Lieberman: I wish we could take credit for the line, "I don't always drink beer, but when I do, I prefer Dos Equis," but Jeff Kling wrote it. Brandon and I were having trouble finding a way to finish the spot. To show this guy being awesome for 25 seconds and then have him say he only drank Dos Equis at the end wasn't really working within the spirit of the idea. We figured we needed to think of a more unusual way to deliver the standard sales pitch and Jeff had that solution. I imagine this is why he makes so much money.

As for the tagline, it was one of the last things we figured out. We worked on two directions: The first direction was to describe Dos Equis and this idea of "interesting" in a creative way. We burned through a lot of taglines. For a while it was "Twice As Interesting As Brand X." And at one point, I seem to even remember presenting a line that was something like, "If you don't find this beer interesting, I will punch you in the face." Heineken didn't like that one.

The second direction was to come up with a tagline that was more aspirational—a point of view that both the brand and the consumer could share. Something like "Just Do It" or "Think Different," but for beer.

"Stay Thirsty" was basically an amalgamation of two idioms: "Thirsting for adventure" and "Staying hungry" and it seemed to work. We added on the "my friends" part to give it a little humanity and levity.

Brandon Henderson: It's funny to think how much harder it was to sell the idea of using an older man as their spokesperson than it was to sell the idea of having him say he didn't always drink their product.

VIDEO GAMES MOVE PAST CUT SCENES AND DEATH METAL: HALO 3 "BELIEVE"

In 2008, the campaign for Halo 3 called "Believe" swept the awards circuit, winning everything, including two Cannes Grand Prix.

The campaign centered on a stunning 90-second film that took viewers on a tour of an epic battle scene, circa 2500, the camera lingering over the fallen bodies and anguished faces of soldiers, burning wrecks, fearsome aliens and finally the hero, Master Chief, the central character in the Halo game series. The battle scene wasn't computer generated though; it was a 1,200-square-foot diorama created by Stan Winston, which gave the piece a monumental historical feel, which is exactly what Believe's creators had in mind. The campaign also included a site created by AKQA that allowed visitors to take a more detailed interactive tour of the scene, complete with 360-degree panoramas and extra information about the weapons and characters in the game. Additional films depicted war veterans in the Museum of Humanity, recalling the battle and paying homage to The Chief.

The campaign was spearheaded by McCann-affiliated agency T.A.G. Creative directors Scott Duchon, Geoff Edwards and John Patroulis, art directors Nate Able and Tim Stier and copywriter Mat Bunnell enticed a new group of gamers by exploiting the epic storytelling aspect of the game, with Master Chief as a more humanized, classic hero.

SCOTT DUCHON ON THE MAKING OF BELIEVE

On Halo 3 we literally had three different briefs:

First, there were the hardcore gaming fans—there were six million of them and they were probably going to buy the game anyway, so it was a matter of just not pissing them off.

The next ring out was the million or so people who are gamers who just haven't bought Halo. How do you get them involved at the end of the trilogy?

The third circle was entertainment enthusiasts. They want to be part of something big in culture. They're the people who go to see blockbuster films. We have to introduce them to gaming. They have to buy the game AND the console. So we need this to feel important and big, but there needs to be an emotional thing that connects those segments together. That's where the idea of Master Chief as a figure of heroism comes in. It would be something that Halo fans could relate to, and for the people in between, it was something to get them to ask what they have been missing out on. It all came down to an emotional kind of thing. We thought about it from a historical perspective: how have heroes been looked at and celebrated? From the dawn of time there were stories that were told. Then they turned into songs and tapestries. Then they became books and monuments and statues. Then there were films. We asked, what would it look like in the future?

We started to talk about how we don't really have heroes in modern times. They are sport celebrities or they're fictional characters. You don't see many statues erected to these guys. We had a couple of teams doing concepts for this. One of the art directors came in and said, "How about a giant diorama?" That became the starting point. The other team came up with the idea of films from people who survived the battle. Those were separate; it was almost two ideas at the same time. The diorama became the center of the campaign. We wanted to build it for real so people could fly through it.

It wasn't the first time that Duchon and his crew broke from convention in a campaign for a successful video game. A year earlier, T.A.G. had been charged with launching the highly anticipated Cliff Bleszinski creation Gears of War. A third-person shooter, featuring a cast of preternaturally large soldiers sporting weapons like the Hammer of Dawn and doing battle with the Locust Horde, the game oozed testosterone from its every pixel:

So T.A.G. created a spot with virtually no violent gunplay. The gorgeous dark visuals, created by director Joseph Kosinski and Digital Domain using the game engine itself, featured GOW protagonist Marcus Fenix having a pensive moment surveying the destruction around him against the kind of poignant, introspective soundtrack typically reserved for break-up scenes in *The Hills*. The track in this case was Gary Jules's extra-moody cover of "Mad World," and it set the tone for the rest of the GOW campaigns from that point. The game went on to sell 2 million copies in six weeks (as of 2008 it had sold nearly 6 million copies), making it the best selling game until . . . Halo 3.

As far as putting ideas out there, I've always tried to take a bit of a chance. There was a formula to making video game commercials; edit together some cut scenes from the game, put a rocking track on it, maybe some Nickelback. It was so cliché. And it wasn't giving the consumer any credit. It was, "this is what they buy so let's keep doing it." I thought, what if we took a chance, maybe we tell a story, maybe it's an emotional story. I mean, look at them [the GOW characters]; they look like they're on 15 cycles of steroids—what could be more emotional? But there is storytelling to the game, there's a plot, there is more to it and there is more to the target. So what if you just open the aperture a little bit more. Obviously we chose to put a song on there that really resonated with people. There are times you get lucky and we did. I presented the commercial with that song, it wasn't like we found it later; it was always part of the idea. We tried a different take and it worked. Even Cliffy B [the game's creator, Cliff Bleszinski] recognizes the marketing as a huge part of what the brand has become. When Cliffy went on the Jimmy Fallon show, he showed the film we did for Gears. He didn't show cut scenes; he showed our film.

Then it becomes about trying not to repeat yourself in other things you do. It's good when you have clients and creatives saying, "I don't want to repeat THAT. Let's look over to the right a little further." It's an exciting time now with content and how it lives and how people are helping to create it themselves. Everyone wants to come up with ideas; it feels like a rejuvenation.

LETTING THE AUDIENCE TELL THE STORY:
OASIS, *"DIG OUT YOUR SOUL* IN THE STREETS"

In September 2008, agency BBH New York and NYC and Company, New York's marketing and tourism body, sent a group of 15 street musicians and bands into New York subways to play as yet unreleased songs from the forthcoming Oasis album, *Dig Out Your Soul*.

Musicians rehearsed from secret encrypted files of the songs, then on September 12, 2008, gathered in a Brooklyn loft to go over the tracks with their creators, Noel and Liam Gallagher, and then dispersed to entertain unsuspecting New Yorkers with the reinterpreted songs. Web articles, press releases and Google Maps directed people to the concert venues, and fans were encouraged to post their own pictures and videos online. BBH and directing team The Malloys captured the process and the performances for promotional videos and an eventual 18-minute documentary that was released a month later on the band's MySpace page.

Over 250,000 people watched the 18-minute documentary in the first week after its release. *Dig Out Your Soul* became the band's first top-ten release in years. The campaign went on to win a Titanium Lion, a Gold One Show pencil, the top prize at the Andy Awards, the Grandy and other awards.

The campaign was the creation of Calle and Pelle Sjoenell, ECDs at BBH New York, under Chief Creative Officer Kevin Roddy and working with producer Julian Katz.

CALLE AND PELLE SJOENELL ON THE CREATION OF
DIG OUT YOUR SOUL IN THE STREETS

Pelle Sjoenell: Calle and I were appointed creative leaders of the NYC & Company business to promote tourism for New York. They always had an open brief. The thinking was, the city is too great to put into an ad; let's look at the city as an ad. At the same time we were looking at the music industry. We said, OK, who's in trouble? And the music industry certainly was at the time. We were inspired by Radiohead, who had recently done their album launch where you could pay anything. We wanted to come up with something that was more about the music. If you think about what happened traditionally to a music launch, to a song as it traveled through all the filters of success, if it was successful, it got played on the radio, then it got into high rotation on MTV and maybe if they were lucky, eventually someone sang their song in karaoke and then someone makes a living playing the song in the street. We reversed it. The campaign was an interactive trailer for what the songs could be. We took it to NYC and they loved it and we talked to Warner Bros. Music who brought in Oasis, who at the time wanted to make more of an impact in the U.S. For them it was important to have a credible realness about them. When they came to the U.S., they could have made a music video showing them running around New York making high-fives around SoHo. Instead they did this. They made a real connection with real musicians. It was an homage to American street music; that was the thinking behind it.

Calle Sjoenell: The interesting part of it was that the people who participated in it, they took it upon themselves to spread it and tell their version of the story. Of course the musicians who participated said "whoa we're here with Oasis" and they brought their own videographers and people who blogged about it. They started promoting it, fans who were here wrote about it on fan forums and posted pictures to a Flickr group. The idea spread organically.

Pelle: We also learned a lot from this experiment about how to think of target groups in different ways. People talk about a target audience, but you also have to figure out what your target's target is. Who are they talking to? Fans talk to other fans and they're our actual target. The first target is bounced to the next one. Before, when you created a message, you figured out who was receiving it and then, OK you check them off. But that's not enough now. It's great that someone saw it, but how do you make them want to promote it or be a part of it?

IDEA-FIRST INTEGRATION:
THE MINI LAUNCH CAMPAIGN

LET'S SIP, NOT GUZZLE. *Let's leave the off-road vehicles off road. Let's stop pretending we live in the jungle. Let's stop intimidating each other. Let's not use the size of our vehicle to compensate for other short-*

comings. Let's reclaim our garage space. Let's be nimble. Let's be quick. Let's be honest. LET'S MOTOR.

When the Mini debuted in the United States in 2002, it was a genuine head turner. Though SUV sales were just about to peak, "bigger is better" was still the prevailing automotive aesthetic. Trucks, SUVs and minivans made up six of the top ten best-selling vehicles in 2002.[3]

The sight of what was then the relatively tiny and feisty-looking ride elicited a visceral reaction from onlookers.

Crispin Porter+Bogusky provoked and harnessed that reaction in the groundbreaking campaign it created to launch the BMW-owned brand in America.

Working with a marketing budget that matched the car's stature, CP+B eschewed the traditional big-car TV blowout in favor of innovative print and outdoor initiatives. Over the course of the campaign, the agency fastened Minis to the top of SUVs and drove them across the country, put Minis in the seats at stadiums, and created Mini supermarket rides, with giant price tags attached.

The agency invented whole new categories of magazine advertising, creating a double-page spread on which the Mini appeared to be cornering around the binding staples, and incorporating the car into the ongoing "Batboy" narrative on the cover of the legendary *Weekly World News*. It made long-copy outdoor billboards that outlined the brand's manifesto ("Let's put away the middle finger. Let's lay off the horn. Let's volunteer jumper cables. Let's pay a stranger's toll . . ."). It also created a "Book of Motoring."

The campaign was created by then–creative director Andrew Keller (now co-CCO) and a team of writers and creatives that initially included Bill Wright, Tony Calcao, Rob Strasberg, Tom Adams, Mark Taylor and Ari Merkin (who left the agency shortly after the campaign broke) and expanded over the years to include many others.

The Mini launch earned endless accolades for its inventive ads, but the core of the campaign was a philosophy, what Keller calls a cultural line in the sand, summed up by the campaign tag line, "Let's Motor."

It was one of the best examples to date of media and creativity as one thought, of the integrated idea-first campaign, and it became one of the most influential campaigns in modern advertising.

It also, says Keller, exemplified the agency's "cultural tension" approach and highlighted the importance of generosity and a good thesaurus.

ANDREW KELLER ON CREATING LET'S MOTOR

It was the smallest car in America. It seemed like we had the opportunity to create this new culture of driving. We looked at driving culture, and it seemed broken. It seemed that other modes of going had a better culture, whether that was boats, motorcycles, etc. This car was unique enough, it had enough things that made it iconic and alternative to what was out there, which granted it the sort of soapbox to create this new culture of going. A new, enlightened culture of going was how we talked about it.

And so it became, what are the components of this culture, what do we call this culture, how do we define this culture?

We were looking for a call to action. I think all great tag lines are a call to action; they're a call to something bigger. It's not just "hey, buy this product," but a call to something more transcendent or philosophical. That's the way I think great tag lines work. We wanted ours to be a call to this product and a call to this culture—take a different approach to life and to driving. That was the genesis of Let's Motor. It actually came out of a thesaurus. We were looking at "going" and "go" and the word motor was in there. It was perfect and it had a nice tie-in to the Britishness of the car. We knew the car was being made by Germans, but we didn't want it to be about BMW. We wanted to create a modern personality that was an icon unto itself, but it wasn't unreasonable to borrow some British attitude. The brand wasn't overly British anymore and we didn't want to hang our hats on that. But "motor" was a great term; it was a different sort of driving, it was slightly odd. It's good if a tag line clanks a little bit, if it uses words differently for the time but is of the time.

There was some research that said that some people didn't get "Let's Motor," that they thought it was like saying "Let's Engine." But culturally it was let's motor, let's get the fuck out of here, or let's hurry. It gave us a spectrum of meaning.

It was about the relationship between you and the road, the relationship between you and other drivers, it was about being OK if the car gets dirty. A lot of what motoring principles were about was turning convention on its head and all of that was then put together in "The Book of Motoring," which tried to lay out that philosophy. The other element of it was what I've been calling generosity. Which is like saying you don't necessarily have to buy our product. For example, Twelpforce [the Twitter-based customer service campaign the agency created for retailer Best Buy, where the stores' staffers answered prospective customers' tweets directly]. We're offering you customer service; you may use it and then go buy somewhere else. There's a certain generosity there that people ultimately reciprocate; they want to work with you. Part of that philosophy was that you don't have to have a Mini to motor. Of course it makes it easier, and it's a philosophy we created and stand for, but to motor you can just do these things—take a different route to work, don't get stuck in a rut, have a more creative approach to driving. It was really about this other way of going.

We came into a marketplace with such a different product, a marketplace where people loved SUVs; the Mini stood against everything America stood for. A lot of brands try and reconcile their product to the reigning culture; if it's something small, they would say, "Well, it's bigger than you think." That's why it was important to create our own culture, to make an effort to change the way people thought about things, rather than say, "Hey, we fit into your culture, you just have to look at us differently."

"The Book of Motoring" came about as we were studying driving conventions and car culture conventions and then started turning those things on their heads. As we started looking at those things, we started to say, "Hey, this is a great opportunity for a book to come out of all this."

What's interesting is that we had originally developed a different line for Mini. We had presented the strategy with the line "It Lives." The idea that this car had a life of its own. That was a whole other side to this conversation, which was making Mini an icon. That was the goal because one of the characteristics of an icon is that they create an emotional response. Everyone had this response to Mini when they saw it. The notion was we could anthropomorphize it. That's the genesis of some of the campaign ideas, like having the Mini in a stadium. But that's where we felt like that was only about the car. In reality, we kept working on it, and it was literally days before the final presentation where we switched it to "Let's Motor" and made it about the book. We pulled all that together and went in with something different knowing they loved "It Lives."

On the Campaign

It was very important not to behave like other car companies. You can't really run a TV spot that says we're different from other car companies; if you do that, you're doing what every car company does. That was part of the decision, and money was a part of that decision; we had a limited budget. We looked at magazines, but we wanted media that were going to generate conversation and magazines don't really do that. People don't say, "Did you see that ad in that magazine?" We don't assume people are looking at the same magazines we are. So thinking about how we were going to create a buzz around magazines, that's where the idea of doing inserts came from. We wanted people to take it out of the magazine and pass it around. We also wanted to have the conversation where the culture was happening, which was part of the reason that outdoor was something we embraced. Outdoor is a great spot for iconic brands. People sense that it's a brand that shouts from the mountaintop to everyone. TV is similar, but even TV is targeted based on the show. Outdoor is not targeted; it's an iconic medium and a great car culture medium. That led us to long-copy outdoor boards. It challenged the convention of outdoor, purposely. People would have to slow down to read part of it on the way to work. They were forced to have to deal with it and debate it. And that would establish it as an alternative voice.

There were so many awesome copywriters that worked on it. Bill Wright was a huge writer on that, Steve O'Connell, especially around the book of motoring. Ari Merkin was really the one I remember. I was sitting in my office, and it was late in the process. Really the whole thing was about what we were going to do, not what we were going to say. We had these insert things, things people could play with, we wanted people to interact with the brand. Ari came in and hands me this thing and it was just "Let's . . ." "Let's . . ." "Let's . . ." it was all the repetition, all these calls to action, all these ideas for people to engage in and inspiring thoughts. I was like, "That's it." Ari was an important contributor in terms of creating that repetitive cadence of "Let's . . ."

On Cultural Tension

To me, tension is what attracts attention. It's really about creating a clear line between two things that forces discussion. When it comes down to it, I guess the way I internalize it is, would anyone talk about it? Does it feel like we're drawing a line in the sand, have we created a notion, are we solving a problem, are we creating an enemy? The way we attempt to resolve that tension is to talk about it.

The important part of tension is that it is relevant to culture. You have to uncover what the relevance of a product is, why people are going to talk about it. The best example of tension for Mini was the billboard that said "The SUV backlash officially starts now."

It was drawing a line in the sand: there's driving and there's motoring. It implied you need to make a decision.

Tension can be a negative word, but in the sense of driving culture, it was more positive: "let's put away the middle finger." It was a call to something more optimistic. I mean, there was no getting around the fact that the car was a smile-generating machine.

THE IDEA/TV CAMPAIGN/ SOCIAL MEDIA PHENOMENON: OLD SPICE "THE MAN YOUR MAN COULD SMELL LIKE"

I'm on a horse.

Whichever way you looked at it, 2009 was a tough year. Wall Street had well and truly buggered everyone, the economy was in ruins, marketers' budgets and appetite for risk had shrunk to new lows, and agencies shed thousands of jobs. While a few brands capitalized on the down market and took the opportunity to connect with people in a new way, most hunkered down.

It was a bad year for spots, too; at the risk of sounding like one of those calcified curmudgeons from chapter 6, there really did seem to be fewer really good ones than usual. This was, in a way, a good thing. It meant that the industry had finally really branched out and was expressing itself in a riot of new ways—apps, events, content and new and better uses of social media abounded.

Production company sources actually reported that good agencies—those that had adapted to the times and had been producing a variety of digital work—had started to lament that they had lost their spot-making mojo.

And then, in the early days of 2010, the spot gauntlet was thrown down, hard. Wieden+Kennedy Portland's "The Man Your Man Could

Smell Like" hit the cultural consciousness like a bracing slap of alcohol-based cologne on freshly shaved cheeks.

There was no elaborate set-up, no cool music, no sweeping cinematography. The spot had a disarming immediacy. A hunky man wearing only a towel addressed the camera, and the audience, directly.

"Hello ladies."

Well hello.

What came next were 17 words that put the commercials-making world on notice and launched tens of millions of web views, media impressions, parodies and, later, a seismic social media initiative.

"Look at your man, now back to me. Now back at your man; now back to me."

The man in the towel, played by former NFL wide receiver Isaiah Mustafa, is encouraging the ladies to have their men use Old Spice body wash instead of more feminine alternatives. He is supremely confident, authoritative and completely adorable.

As he speaks . . .

> Sadly he isn't me. But if he stopped using lady-scented body wash and switched to Old Spice, he could smell like he's me.
>
> Look down; back up. Where are you? You're on a boat with the man your man could smell like.
>
> What's in your hand? Back at me. I have it. It's an oyster with two tickets to that thing you love. Look again; the tickets are now diamonds. Anything is possible when your man smells like Old Spice and not a lady.
>
> I'm on a horse.

. . . he moves seamlessly from his bathroom shower to a boat to a beach or, rather, his backgrounds move seamlessly to reflect his monologue.

The combination of the unusual structure of his speech, the eye-popping single-take transitions that appear to be done without CG tricks and, well, the man himself made the spot impossible to skip.

W+K had already made a dent in Old Spice's deadly "mature" image. When the agency won ad duties for the P&G brand in 2006, it immediately launched a campaign featuring the suave cult favorite Bruce Campbell, singing the praises of experience. It was a funny and effective way to refresh the brand's image and erase some grandfatherly associations—the product says "Old" right on the package, for Christ's sake—while not pretending that it was Axe.

A string of well-received spots and web efforts followed. But TMYMCSL was something else. The spot was viewed over 17 million times online, and media outlets from *People* to Oprah trumpeted its excellence. A string of parodies, some of them startlingly good, followed. This was the commercial that the stranger sitting next to you on the plane, your hairdresser, your aunt talked about. The Old Spice man had done what spots were no longer supposed to be able to do— it became a mass cultural touchstone.

The spot's creators, Eric Kallman and Craig Allen, were the same duo who had helped create the radically excellent Skittles campaign while at TBWA\Chiat\Day New York a few years earlier, authoring spots like "Piñata" and "Touch." Their sensibilities were shaped in the unnatural world of candy, and they had honed their skills cranking out countless scripts for their exacting Chiat\Day bosses, Ian Reichenthal, Scott Vitrone and Gerry Graf—Kallman says the team wrote 280 scripts to get to "Piñata."

Kallman and Allen are copywriter and art director, respectively, but in name only. The team has worked as a unit writing all the spots they've done.

Allen says the team's creative process is remarkably . . . silent. No gratuitous bantering, no jibber jabber. If somebody speaks up, it means there's something important that's bubbled up.

Unsurprisingly, given the team's pedigree, they also follow the dumb rule: "If it's dumb, it's probably good." Which means there's nothing forced; if an idea strikes one of them as original enough to be dumb, then there's probably something to it.

The brief for Old Spice body wash was simple—women buy a lot of bath and shower products for their households, so appeal to women. And any Old Spice brief came with an additional creative constraint—it had to revolve around a man speaking to the camera, a construct that the marketer favored.

"So, there's not that many ways to do that," says Kallman.

> The hardest part was, how do we do that, but not alienate the dudes. We were sitting there, it was late at night and we didn't have anything we loved yet; thanks to working for Scott and Ian we push ourselves really hard.

So we had some other ideas and thought that it would be cool if, instead of just looking at the camera and talking, he was talking more directly with the viewer. And then that became, what if we did something where the guy is speaking that directly just to women. The ideas before had been kind of that he was speaking to everyone. And so we were just trying to be quiet, staring at each other like usual. And out of nowhere, Craig said, "Hello ladies, look at your man, now back at me." And I laughed. And we rarely ever say something where the other one laughs.

Allen says they constructed the rest of the spot fairly quickly after that. "We did the whole spot and we were kind of laughing at just the dialog. But we didn't really know what we were going to show. The first time we presented the script, I don't even know if we presented it with visuals, which is really weird for us because everything we work on is so visual. But, when we finished we were just kind of like, well, did we just write a radio spot?"

Which led to the idea, says Allen, that is counter to what every copywriter learns in school, to show exactly what the dialogue was saying. "But we were like, it's so stupid that it might work," says Allen.

"I'm on a horse," incidentally, was not in the original script. It was added after the fact, in production. "It was that random, which is why I think it works; we didn't put too much thought into it," says Allen.

The crucial one-take look of the visuals was also not scripted; the team had thought about it, but not included it in the script. Director and frequent collaborator Tom Kuntz ended up suggesting the one-take approach anyway and worked out the whole brilliant choreography of getting The Man from bathroom to horseback.

It was the first time the team ever wrote a spot dialog first. "We just usually think of an idea that fits the brief and then it usually entails characters talking to each other or some kind of spokesperson speaking, or something. That just comes as part of it. But we had never sat down and written a paragraph of dialog first." This time, says Kallman, "We literally just wrote the lines so we had one that made us laugh and we literally worked the first line of the plot."

Several months and one Cannes Film Grand Prix later, The Man was back in another one-shot wonder called "Questions." The spot had the same ultra-masculine appeal to the ladies, an even more elaborate series of in-camera transitions and a killer catch phrase ("swan dive!"). What came next was, unbelievably, even better, and immediately made every social media guru hate himself for not thinking of it first.

Starting on July 13, 2010, the Old Spice man began responding directly to comments made about the spot on Twitter, Facebook, YouTube and sites like Reddit. Each bespoke video response featured Mustafa, in his trademark towel, speaking from what appeared to be his bathroom, directly to the commenter in his hypnotic baritone. He responded to internet celebrities—like Ashton Kutcher, Guy Kawasaki, Biz Stone of Twitter, Alyssa Milano, and Digg founder Josh Rose—and nobodies alike. Each response felt painstakingly crafted, though it was written, filmed, edited and posted on the fly. And each response was received with sheer delight from recipients and duly Tweeted and posted on Facebook, begetting more views and more comments to be responded to.

As Writer/Creative Director Jason Bagley told *Creativity*,

> We had a kind of NASA control center about 15 feet away from Isaiah at two different tables. At one table were Josh Millrod, Dean McBeth and Cody Corona, interactive community managers and digital strategists who were going through all the comments and monitoring all web activity. They were selecting the comments to respond to. Eric Baldwin, Eric Kallman, Craig Allen and I sat at another table furiously writing the responses. We would pass our computers back and forth to one another, checking one another's work and adding jokes to one another's copy. The four of us took turns directing. In another room was a team of editors cranking out everything we shot. Not to mention the entire production crew of camera, lighting, teleprompter worker person, etc.

In the end, the W+K team made nearly 200 response videos over the course of two days.

The results were staggering—on its first day, the responses got nearly 6 million views on YouTube and by day three had surpassed 20 million views. One week after launch, the videos had been viewed 40 million times, making Old Spice the most viewed branded YouTube channel ever. According to W+K, the whole campaign has generated 1.4 billion media impressions. And the money shot—in the month after the "Responses" went live, Old Spice sales were up 107 percent.

The social media coup was the brainchild of Iain Tait, the interactive creative director who co-founded digital agency Poke in London and who joined W+K in 2010 in the role of global interactive creative director. Tate is a high-profile industry presence; his popular CrackUnit blog is a favorite among digital types, but he was also accomplished in using social media in meaningful ways for brands. His agency's Baker Tweet was an early example of a Twitter-based brand utility—it was a device that allowed London's Albion Bakery to tell what goodies were freshest from the oven with the flip of a switch.

Tait says his job at W+K is to "push the agency to use technology to connect people, culture and brands in interesting ways." And he wasted no time doing so.

The "Responses" effort showed the world how real-time, conversational interactive marketing was done.

Without a playbook, the agency invented a new way to join the cultural discussion taking place every minute across the social media landscape and do it in a way that was welcome, and in a way that harmonized with the overall campaign idea and had an unmistakable yet not overbearing brand connection.

It was a particularly sweet victory for W+K, which had suffered a bad rap for not being "digital enough" years earlier when founding client Nike took a piece of its business to another agency (that piece wasn't gone long, it returned to the agency a year later). Just a month prior to the launch of the Responses effort, the agency had won the Cannes Cyber Grand Prix for its "ChalkBot" project for Nike (a machine that chalked consumer's Tweeted words of encouragement on the Tour de France course), and now it had a social media case study that will sit alongside previous groundbreakers like BMW Films and Subservient Chicken.

IAIN TAIT TALKS ABOUT THE INVENTION

I was incredibly lucky, I walked into a meeting on a piece of business where the client, the agency, a performer and the audience were all in perfect alignment.

The Old Spice Guy was already a huge online character through the two previous ads. I hesitate a little to call them ads because they'd kind of transcended that and become content. At that point they'd had nearly 20 million views online and millions more in traditional media.

Those views and all the comments and tweets about them effectively created a test bed and an environment that we could mine to find fans, influencers and communities that we could engage with for the launch of the Responses campaign. So we were hitting the ground running.

And not only that, but here was a character whose performance was based on him looking straight into the audience's eyes. Talking directly to camera about the product in a way that people adore. An advertiser's dream.

Plus we had a set of great writers and a performer who were all so excited and buzzed about what they were doing that they had absolutely no fear about the prospect of creating new content in real time.

When you look at it, how could you not have come up with the idea of doing response videos?

Why Was Responses Embraced to Such a Degree?

Great writing, great performances, a great behind-the-scenes team, smart social media seeding and reactions. It was the fact that all of those people were working together as a single team with a seamless handover between all parts of the process. There were no silos and no divisions—everyone was just working flat out to make it work.

The fact that everyone was having fun shouldn't be underestimated. And because speed was so important to the success of the idea, things weren't able to be overthought and overprocessed. It was honest, joyful and from the gut. Which is pretty rare in advertising these days.

BRAND UTILITY:
FIAT ECO:DRIVE

AKQA, the digital agency that created the online complement to Halo 3 "Believe's" diorama, has been behind some of the highest-profile interactive campaigns of the last several years. In 2008, the agency created something that transcended the idea of interactive marketing with eco:Drive, an app for automaker Fiat.

The app, working with in-car technology developed with Microsoft called Blue & Me, helps users mine driving data with an eye to promoting more efficient driving and reducing fuel consumption and emissions. Drivers download the eco:Drive Adobe AIR app, load it onto a USB stick and then plug the stick into the Blue & Me port in their Fiat. When the data is uploaded back onto users' computers, the app calculates the drivers' efficiency index from things like acceleration, deceleration, speed and gear shifting and then recommends more efficient on-road habits.

Like Nike+ two years earlier, eco:Drive was an example of brand utility.

As The Barbarian Group's Benjamin Palmer told *Ad Age* in 2006, "The big change that needs to happen is that we need, as an industry, to be innovators in making ourselves useful. . . . For the same budget and energy as we expend on current forms of advertising, we could be making something more tangible, useful and reusable that plays a more integral part in the consumer's life."

Actually, it's usually less budget. Remember, many big marketers devote tens of millions of dollars to "media." Today, when some of the best brand communications can be distributed without million-dollar TV campaigns, what if those millions were redirected to actually creating great things?

eco:Drive has been one of the interesting answers.

According to AKQA chief creative officer James Hilton, since its launch in October 2008, eco:Drive has been rolled out across eleven Fiat models, translated into nine languages and been developed for fleet managers. More than 100,000 users have downloaded the application, and drivers have saved 3,000 tons of CO_2 (equivalent to a jumbo jet flying from London to New York 8,500 times) and have collectively saved £3 million ($4.6 million) worth of fuel.

AKQA LONDON CHIEF CREATIVE OFFICER JAMES HILTON ON ECO:DRIVE

Fiat eco:Drive was an idea; no brief. No brainstorm (no one should ever have to sit through a brainstorm). It was an idea born from the necessity of needing to make things better. Fiat had recently installed Microsoft's Blue & Me, the USB technology, into their vehicles. Primarily, the purpose of these was to enable drivers to upload MP3s

BRINGING IDEAS TO LIFE

177

into the car's entertainment system; however, Fiat had established that driving data could be retrieved via the same device. They used it as a helpful shortcut to access the vehicle's diagnostics. Which did rather beg the question: "If we know what the car is doing and how it's being driven based on this data, can we use it to help people become better drivers?" Plug in. Drive. Unplug. Into PC. Hey presto. Easy. Sort of. You see the tricky thing about making technology easy is, it isn't.

The essence of eco:Drive was to make sense of all this data and turn it into something useful. In the beginning, however, all we had was a mass of numbers and variables. A data blob, if you will. AKQA's job was to work with Fiat engineers to understand and define which data sets would be useful, and which would not. Fiat and AKQA technologists began the initial task of devising algorithms that would shape the data into a useful form. In parallel to this, AKQA was developing a look and feel for the concept of "eco:Drive," and to find its tone of voice that would help define the project and transform the complex into the simple. Although I'm pretty sure most companies would tell you they were running "parallel work-streams in order to harness productivity and create a collaborative working environment," it would be closer to the truth to say we were making it up as we went along. This is why eco:Drive was so hugely exciting to work on, for Fiat and for AKQA. We were in uncharted waters, deciding which way the project should take us and ultimately being led by the extraordinary technological achievements of the joint AKQA/Fiat teams.

But, as they say, technology is only of any use when it becomes invisible. And this was nowhere more true than for eco:Drive. Turning hard data into a tangible, helpful and enjoyable experience for a driver was key. At AKQA, we run all our projects with three words in mind: Useful. Usable. Delightful. These three words are the cornerstones of any engaging product; you can apply them to a vase, a bin, a phone or a car. In this case it was software.

Useful in this case was the way in which the eco:Drive application analyzes your acceleration, deceleration, gear changes and speed. It then awards you a mark out of 100, according to how efficiently you have driven. Usable was the word of the day when it came to step-by-step tutorials to help you improve your score, providing practical advice on how to perfect your driving style. The tone of voice was explanatory without being superior and friendly without being condescending. And finally, delight came in the shapes of

Franco, Merv and Claudia, three animated employees of Fiat acting as demonstrators and guides to the system.

The key to eco:Drive's success has been its "human" approach to an "engineering" idea. Making environmental and automotive information easy, even enjoyable, to understand. It uses technologies that people are already familiar with and it helps by showing how they can improve their driving. It shows them how better driving translates into lower emissions. And lastly, and arguably most tangibly, it demonstrates how much money they are saving by following eco:Drive's advice. Not bad for a USB key.

ICONS:
DAVID ABBOTT AND THE *ECONOMIST* CAMPAIGN

Many of the campaigns here were created in the digital age. This one wasn't. But it had all the hallmarks of an engaging campaign that transcended a single medium and became part of popular culture, a campaign that was parodied and appropriated and reinterpreted and that endures still.

The *Economist* poster campaign was created by David Abbott, the legendary copywriter who had worked at the famed DDB of Bill Bernbach in the 1960s and who launched Abbott Mead Vickers in London in 1978. In 1991, the agency became Abbott Mead Vickers BBDO.

Abbott shaped an era in advertising, but his influence was global. He was best known for his print work, like the Volvo ad depicting a car suspended over his own sweet self with the headline, "If the welding isn't strong enough, the car will fall on the writer"[4] and uncomfortably direct ads for the RSPCA.

In a 2003 piece in U.K. trade *Campaign*, adman Robin Wight asked, by way of examining the increasingly visual orientation of advertising, "Would David Abbott Get a Job in Advertising Today?"[5]

Abbott, who retired in 1999, and recently wrote a novel, *The Upright Piano Player* (to be released in the United States in 2010) thinks he would.

DAVID ABBOTT ON THE *ECONOMIST* CAMPAIGN

We pitched for the *Economist* account. At the first meeting, I didn't want us to take the account. Media accounts could be difficult; journalists think they know how to write better than copywriters do, and maybe they're right.

You have to deal with the publisher and the editor, the work is usually intensive and there are small budgets and last-minute deadlines. So after our chemistry meeting, I thought, this will probably not be worth doing.

We withdrew from the pitch, but the client was insistent. He said, "We've decided to appoint you." For a year we did pretty conventional advertising, which had to be approved by 17 people at *The Economist* before it could run. It was everything I thought it would be at the start.

It was not really a campaign and not really branded in a strong way; they felt that, and I felt that. When the next season's work came around, I was sitting at my desk one day, and I noticed that the shape of the *Economist* logo was the same proportion as a 48 sheet poster. I thought posters would be a different way of advertising that kind of magazine.

I thought pragmatically that since they don't have detailed body copy, they'd be easier to get past the vetting process. But overall, I thought we should see *The Economist* as a brand, as a positioning, rather than the traditional approach of advertising a magazine's contents, and a poster seemed an opportunity to do that. I hit on the idea of red simply because I thought that would be strong branding, and red was something they were using. I wanted to make *The Economist* a club that you wanted to belong to, a club of the intelligent-stroke-successful so even if people didn't read it they might come to think it was a badge of honor. There was also a technical reason—basically *The Economist* depended on attracting ABC1 readers;[6] they marketed that fact to advertisers. It wasn't easy to reach ABC1 males. One of the magazine's biggest selling tools was its annual surveys on readership profiles. We had to find a way of keeping the ABC content high in those profiles.

The tone of it just came, I think, because if you say literally, "read this and be successful," it's crass. But if you say "I never read the *Economist*" (management trainee, aged 42), it's charming. So we adopted that tone. For the first showing we printed the posters up so they saw something that looked like the finished article. I have to say it was an easier sell. They loved it immediately. David Gordon, the chief executive, was jumping up and down. It was one of the best meetings I ever had.

We did two campaigns a year with six or seven executions in each. We never repeated to create anticipation and excitement. People looked for the next one. As we went along we did things like ads on top of buses [the buses that cruised the streets of London, so people looking down from office towers would see the message: "Hello to our readers in high office"].

For the first couple of years, I wrote all of them, then I wrote some of them, then we opened it up to the whole creative department to create the lines. Some people could do it, and some people couldn't.

When I wrote them, I used to choose a concept; I'd get an idea and then do 50 or 60 headline revisions to get it right. They were harder to do than they looked. They ran for ten or twelve years, then the client decided it had served its purpose, which I think was a mistake. It was their signature. But that's the fate of long-running campaigns; every two or three years, the marketing director changes and a new one comes along and wants to make a name. Clients get tired of advertising much more quickly than the public does. The client sees it every day.

So many campaigns have got more life in them than they're allowed. You have to update long-running campaigns, and you can change the emphasis. We changed the emphasis of *The Economist* campaign. When we ran in the Gordon Gekko period, there was a kind of reaction against the greed of bankers and that sort of association. We subtly switched from talking about success to talking about knowledge and being in the know. I wrote a poster in this time frame that said, "Would you like to sit next to you at dinner?" It was about being interesting and informed. We reacted to the mood of the times, but we didn't abandon the campaign.

The first wave of the campaign was "I never read *The Economist* . . . ," "The edge of a conversation is the loneliest place on earth," "It's lonely at the top but at least there's something to read," "Don't be the vacancy on the board. . . ." We did a few hundred. We had some visual ones—we played tricks and did game-type puzzles. The magazine has always been a punchy read; we tried to reflect that in the advertising.

I remember once David Gordon brought me in a poster his son had written and one that he'd written that he thought was good . . . they wouldn't have got through the agency. I did run one of his, though; on the route from his office to his house, we put up a poster just for him.

The budget was only ever less than a million pounds—a small account but it had an enormous impact. Their readership figure grew, and the campaign was picked up in America.

We took it into TV on occasion. One of my favorite films was the Henry Kissinger commercial. It was a stationary camera inside a plane. There is a man sitting in a seat just before takeoff. And Henry Kissinger gets on and sits next to him. The voiceover says "You're sitting in seat 2B, I wonder who'll be sitting in seat 2A." And it's Henry Kissinger. He says good evening and the VO says "Ready for a good chat?" and the guy slinks down in his seat. We had just an hour with him and he was impatient and inevitably things go wrong and he was not happy and said he had an appointment to get to and couldn't be late. One of the clients was an attractive young woman, and we sent her over to talk to him and all of a sudden his appointment somehow disappeared. He even stood around a while after the shoot. It was an idea that could be transferred into any other medium if you kept the tone of voice right.

The skills of the creative thinker are the same, even in this day and age. You still have to have an idea that will be noticed by a consumer and be persuasive. That takes a particular set of skills starting with intelligence and then you add craft to that. I think if I were starting again I'd still get a job today. . . .

CHAPTER 8

IT'S JUST GETTING GOOD

In 2010, Pepsi took a pass on the Super Bowl.

It wasn't so unusual for a cost-conscious marketer, post-2009 meltdown, to balk at dropping such a giant wad—$2.5 million for one 30-second slot in the 2010 game and another few million to make a spot worthy of the venue—on the annual ad extravaganza.

But this was Pepsi, a brand that had been part of advertising's biggest showcase for 23 years straight and that, like Budweiser and FedEx, had been a marquee player. Pepsi's Super Bowl ads touting the brand's youthful spirit and featuring stars like Michael Jackson, Britney Spears and Cindy Crawford were some of the most iconic in the Super Bowl commercials pantheon.

What made the move more interesting, though, was what Pepsi did instead of advertising in the big game. The marketer diverted its Super Bowl budget—a stunning $20 million—to a daring social media- and social responsibility-driven initiative. The Pepsi Refresh Project was created by agency TBWA\Chiat\Day L.A. and a diverse group of partners as a year-long initiative whereby Pepsi would give grants ranging from $5,000 to $250,000 to grass roots consumer-generated ideas and programs to change the world for the better.

The project, launched January 13, 2010, was based around the site refresheverything.com, where people could submit ideas in six social good categories—health, arts and culture, food and shelter, the planet, neighborhoods and education—and where visitors voted for their favorite idea. By June, Pepsi had funded about 100 projects—

and was well on its way to its goal of awarding $20 million worth of grants.

The project was a giant-ass landmark, for a number of reasons. Pepsi, the brand known for creating expensive commercial spectacles to tout its youth appeal (and for setting Michael Jackson's hair on fire), was diverting its resources to doing something that youth, apparently, actually care about. It was diverting vast sums of money from TV to digital and harnessing social media to build a community-driven platform.

PepsiCo global director-digital and social media Bonin Bough told *Ad Age*: "It's not about digital as its own channel anymore. It's, how do we infuse digital across all of our marketing programs? The first step was socializing the brands and getting all the brands to quickly move away from destination sites and start creating experiences."

As *Ad Age* summed up at the time, "Refresh Project will be closely watched by the industry for its scope and ambition to put digital media at its forefront, its purpose-driven strategy and the way it restructures relationships within Pepsi's agency circle. What Pepsi is trying to accomplish is unprecedented; its philosophy rips up the traditional marketing rulebook."[1]

The brief, says Rob Schwartz, CCO at TBWA\Chiat Day\L.A., was to make Pepsi relevant at a time when the whole carbonated beverage category was in decline.

"We needed a way to get Pepsi back on the cultural landscape," says Schwartz. "We had just launched Refresh as a brand idea. We did a big outdoor effort and Super Bowl ads launching the notion that 'Every generation refreshes the world. Now it's your turn.' This 2.0 of the campaign was going from talking the talk to showing that Pepsi was ready to walk the walk."

When the campaign was being developed in spring of 2009, a number of forces created a kind of virtuous perfect storm, says Schwartz. "There was this whole spirit of giving back that was in the air. Perhaps a kind of after-glow that emanated from the optimism of a new government in Washington . . . combined with the social media revolution. The last piece was the research about Pepsi consumers, and the insights and opportunities that emerged. The research showed that the Pepsi core audience baby boomers—and its potential audience, millennials—had a lot in common. Most notably, both of them had a desire to change the world. And while boomers may have taken action through sit-ins and protests, millennials get their ideas out and organize via the social web."

The original idea, says Schwartz, was built on the notion of a penny-a-can—for every can of Pepsi purchased, a penny goes to the Refresh Project. "Ultimately, this manifested itself in taking the $20 million or so in Super Bowl money and turning it into monthly $1.3 million grants. Other than that, the original idea was kept intact: Every Pepsi Refreshes The World, not just as a slogan, but as real action. Oh, and give people a concrete reason to choose Pepsi over Coke."

A project of this scope also required a perhaps unprecedented level of collaboration between agencies and a new set of players. "The first thing we did was galvanize the team at Pepsi," says Schwartz.

Unlike any idea that had been executed within the company before, the Pepsi Refresh Project touches every part of the organization and we needed to make sure the entire company was aligned. We had representatives from marketing, public relations, legal, sales, consumer affairs, IT, the PepsiCo Foundation, etc., form a board of advisers to help build and guide the idea. This board of advisers still meets monthly to ensure the program is maximized to its full potential within PepsiCo. Once the internal Pepsi team was aligned and enthusiastic, we needed several partners to make the idea a reality. First, we needed people who knew the philanthropy space and we turned to the people at *GOOD* magazine. *GOOD* has served as a terrific adviser letting us know how a big, blue-chip brand could wade in the waters of the do-gooders.

Along with partners Global Giving and Do Something, *GOOD* has also been instrumental in seeing the grants through from award to implementation. That's one part of the story not everyone knows. Each Pepsi Refresh Grant winner is assigned a "caseworker" to help them complete their project. They not only help with financial disbursement, but also provide advice and obtain the proper resources when necessary. We don't just hand out checks. Once the core of the program was built, we turned to HUGE, a digital production company, to help build it. We had digital capabilities at TBWA\Chiat\Day, but we felt it was best to bring on a team that could really dedicate every resource in their company to making sure the website was flawless. And when it came time to launch, there have been few agencies as instrumental as our PR partners, Edelman and Webber Shandwick, whose outreach has helped us garner over 2 billion earned media impressions and counting.

Overall, the project signaled not one but two of the biggest shifts that will happen in marketing in the next era. The first is the shift toward social responsibility as a core assumption for marketers.

The second shift is one forward-looking brand people have been anticipating for years—the reallocation of gargantuan media budgets away from paid media and toward the creation of platforms, products and content

We've seen what Pepsi did with just one year's Super Bowl budget. And remember BMW Films? That project was an early example of a marketer turning the media/production ratio on its head—BMW spent 90 percent of its budget creating show-stopping content and 10 percent on media.

When you think about the marketing budgets of big advertisers—a marketer that's halfway down *Ad Age*'s annual list of 100 leading national advertisers spends over half a billion dollars on media per year—you can start to see how a big shift in this department could change the creative landscape considerably.

Of course big brands—even small brands—will still spend money on paid media. But there is a growing realization that brands have to earn consumers' attention and that perhaps some of that giant media budget should be devoted to doing things that make people's lives better. It might not be rainforest-saving, stray-dog-adopting, cancer-curing better. Maybe it's just a better customer service experience. Maybe it's creating some fantastic content that makes people think or feel instead of cringe. Maybe its making a problem-solving product.

Looking at the possible near futures of marketing and society in general, it's hard to see how brands will not become a bigger part of all of our lives. This is where you, the copywriter, come in.

More brands in more places is a potentially depressing thought, whether your immediate mental leap is to a dystopian *Blade Runner* world of ad blimps and giant geishas, to unfettered corporate greed ultimately wrecking the planet (see BP) or just to a world with more crappy intrusive ads in it.

But here's the good news.

I just saved 15 percent on car insurance.

No, wait (damn you, Geico!). The good news is that all the changes in the media landscape addressed in the previous pages have created more transparency and created a situation in which brands—

and the people working with them—have a very strong impetus to consider the social good, to make things that make sense, that add to people's lives rather than provoke their wrath.

Whether it's Kit Kat using primate-destroying palm oil, United breaking guitars, or Comcast's service standards filling customers with homicidal rage, everything is visible, everything is up for discussion, and consumers are in control of that discussion.

What we're starting to see being borne out again and again is that good service, social responsibility and sustainable practices aren't just for Vermont ice cream makers; they are a collective economic imperative for every kind of company.

As marketers evolve away from just disseminating pre-packaged messages and toward creating longer-term links with consumers, the copywriter's job becomes an almost infinite proposition.

Copywriters and a whole new array of collaborators are, as Bill Bernbach said, "shapers of society," and it is their responsibility to "help lift it onto a higher level."

MARKETING IN AN AGE OF LESS

Rob Schwartz called it a virtuous perfect storm. And at the risk of sounding earnest, there has been a convergence of social and economic factors that have perhaps made more people question the assumptions that have guided their lives—and the brand world—for so long.

The feeling of optimism created by a historic presidential race, the crisis that was wrought when the jaw-dropping (but evolutionarily inevitable) greed of Wall Street and big oil was left to fester and create unstoppable monsters, the chilling economic crash that forced many people to create a new path for themselves and to disassociate their personal identity from the stuff they buy, an internet culture that has made creators and producers of more and more people— these and other factors have combined to create a social and cultural landscape that marketers haven't faced before.

There is the very real possibility of a cultural shift away from the kind of hyper-consumerism that drove American culture for over 60 years, and it will be fascinating to see how that shift will affect marketing and the way marketers approach products and communications.

For decades—for their entire histories, in most cases—marketers created more new things to get people to buy more stuff, spurred on by more advertising. Now, if people start questioning the wisdom of buying more and more stuff and start thinking about buying less, about buying only things that add value, what does advertising do with itself?

There were several articles in 2010 that talked about people turning away from their stuff, about people who had dialed down their consumption, some by choice, some compelled by the recession, and ended up better off. There have been high-profile stories of people who challenged conventional ways of living and buying—like Colin Beavan, a writer who took himself and his family off the grid for a year, living with as small an environmental footprint as possible and documenting the experiment in a book and film called *No Impact Man.*

In 2010, BBH's Heidi Hackemer, the insightful planner quoted earlier in the book, and Fallon's Tamsin Davies launched "Six Items or Less," a contest/experiment that challenged participants to wear only six items of clothing for a month.

Writer and activist Annie Leonard started making a series of animated films called *The Story of Stuff* about the downside of consumerism that have been viewed millions of times.

In the larger marketing space, we've seen the success enjoyed by some of the newer brands that started their lives while some of these changes were in progress—companies like Zappos, built on a cult-like devotion to customer service and being nice, and Etsy, the phenomenally successful ecommerce site for handmade and vintage goods—and that aren't known for advertising at all.

We've also seen agencies start to build their own brands.

Crispin Porter + Bogusky, an agency that has put enormous effort into industrial design and beyond-ad thinking, started working on a bike-sharing program in 2007. Inspired by the public bicycle initiatives in cities like Paris, CP+B created B-Cycle in association with insurance company Humana and Trek bicycles. On Earth Day, April 22, 2010, the program rolled out on the streets of Denver, with 500 B-Cycles at 50 B-stations available as an alternative to cars for short trips.

Not long after, the agency's creative chief Alex Bogusky rolled out too. Bogusky had already stepped away from day-to-day creative duties at the agency in early 2010 and had been working as "chief in-surgent" for MDC, the holding company that owns CP+B. Bogusky had been working more and more on side projects that reflected his growing passions about larger societal issues outside of—and some-times in opposition to—the brand agenda. In 2008, he wrote a weight-loss book called *The 9-Inch Diet,* based on the idea that ex-panding plate and portion sizes were a large part of the American obesity epidemic; more recently, he wrote a lengthy blog post against advertising to children.

He won't be the last creative to struggle with the cognitive disso-nance involved in applying creative energy to selling things.

In its way, it's yet another exciting development. The more cre-ative innovators who are pushing from the outside to keep corpora-tions honest, the more pressure those corporations will face to do the right thing.

Meanwhile, in the years after David Droga invented a new brand to help children around the world gain access to clean water, his agency worked on a number of award-winning projects for brands including Puma, Method and Activision. And in 2008, the agency turned its attention to another modest goal—helping to elect a new president. In 2008, Droga5 worked with the Jewish Council for Edu-cation and Research to create The Great Schlep. The brief: help Obama win the election, which meant helping him clinch key battle-ground states.

The Schlep targeted Florida—specifically the older Jewish de-mographic that was skeptical of the Democratic candidate and that could have swung the election to McCain/(shudder)Palin. Droga5 en-listed comedian Sarah Silverman to star in a video imploring younger Jews to visit their grandparents in Florida and explain that no, Obama wasn't a Muslim and that yes, he was the candidate that they should be backing. Schleppers could sign up for the challenge on the cam-paign site and download a set of talking points to use on bubby and zaidy. The project caught fire in the media. Within weeks, the video was viewed 4 million times, The Great Schlep Facebook group had 25,000 members, and the talking points had been downloaded 1.2 million times. You know the rest of the story.

In the end, Obama received the highest percentage of Florida's Jewish vote in 30 years (78 percent, 351,000 votes) and won Florida by 170,000 votes.

Of course, the Obama campaign had the best social media campaign in political history, eight years of Bush and the terrifying prospect of Sarah Palin a heartbeat away from the presidency going for it. But who knows . . . a copywriter just might have edged a president into power.

Droga himself is bullish on the potential of the new advertising age. "In the last few years I have had more interesting conversations than in the previous 15 combined," he says. "Transparency and consumer control have made our industry so much better. Advertising today has evolved beyond the wrapping paper. Now advertising can shape the actual box. Our ideas can create new product lines, media channels or NGOs. Sure we can sell cars, but we can also help solve global issues. The canvas for our creativity and thinking is far larger than we even realize."

TO SEE THE CAMPAIGNS DISCUSSED IN
THE IDEA WRITERS, VISIT WWW.THEIDEAWRITERS.COM.

AND NOW A FEW WORDS
FROM LEE CLOW

The legendary creative, now global director of media arts for
TBWA Worldwide and chairman of TBWA Media Art Lab,
talks about Apple and the evolution of advertising.

I like to think that more creative business people will be born out of
this era. What we need are entrepreneurs with a creative passion for
building a great brand as opposed to just business logic for building
a brand.

Anyone who has listened to my ranting about media arts has heard
this before, but what's obvious is that people now choose what advertising they want to spend time with and what they want to reject—
what advertising they give a shit about, and what advertising they're
going to click off and ignore. It's become incumbent upon brands or
storytellers or, indeed, anyone who wants to be a part of culture, to be
a hell of a lot more creative than they had to be 20 or 30 years ago.
Creativity has become king. So it's a huge opportunity for storytellers,
content creators or whatever you want to call the people who used to
just write headlines. Now their job is to create stuff that people love
and engage with and respond to and even become disciples of. That's
what's changed—and it's a good thing.

ON APPLE . . .

We have this annoying problem working for Apple, as I told Steve Jobs the other day when he was challenging us on iPad. I said: "Steve, you give us a product that is so amazing that if we do advertising that in any way upstages your product we're doing you a disservice."

At the same time, we found a visual metaphor for iPod and a visual metaphor for Apple and Mac and PC.

Then there's my all-time personal favorite commercial in the history of the world: "Think Different." You know why we got to do Think Different? Because Steve had no product to sell. When he came back to Apple, we had to buy him a year to get the product the way he wanted it, so we got to do a pretty special piece of advertising that was about the brand. If you're telling the story of a brand, you have to be sure you understand what story this brand has to tell. The story Apple has to tell isn't arty-farty creative execution, it's just "Look at this fucking product! It changes everything! Nobody has ever done anything like this before."

When we did "1984," we found a metaphor that people still talk about—that everyone should be able to have the technology. It shouldn't be owned by a leader, it should be democratized. What nobody remembers about the campaign is that we did a dozen executions: we did a 20-page insert, we did six or eight beautiful commercials that demonstrated what the Mac could do, commercials that basically said "it's as easy as this." We introduced people to the mouse and the interface, the icon-based interface. Point and click. The demo commercials were charming and had interesting music and a nice voiceover, and you watched the Mac go through its paces and you saw a baby touch the button at the end. Nobody remembers those, they just remember 1984, but those commercials were the ones that told the story of Mac, and that insert we ran was the most read ad that ever ran in *Fortune*, or wherever it was we ran it. We had incredible readership rates, but the information side of the equation didn't get as much notoriety as the emotional side of the equation.

I think ultimately brands have to do both. They have to have a belief or an emotional point of view, but they also need substance and information to go with the belief. Apple has always come up really big in terms of "OK, where's the proof?" You think technology should be democratized? OK, now everyone has it on their desk and in their house. Jobs kind of has the ability to predict the future, so we never lie when we put our emotional foot forward and we always had the evidence in terms of "show me the money, show me the goods." We could put the product on the table.

When Steve came back to Apple, everything was broken. A lot of people thought they were about to go out of business. They found Jony Ive [head of design at Apple] and eliminated a lot of terrible products and decided to do something great. But he had to buy a year. So we said, let's reengage or reconfirm that the brand is dedicated to a higher purpose. That's when we did "Crazy Ones," the Think Different campaign. It did kind of re-solidify the base. It got some of the software developers who were getting ready to walk away from Apple altogether to reengage. But the highest compliment I've received, maybe in my entire business career, was that Steve said Think Different told the company how to behave. It changed the way Apple came to work every day. How amazing is that to kind of throw down an emotional gauntlet with your storytelling that helps a company to come back from the ashes? Of course, Steve had more to do with it than the ad, but we maybe created the T-shirt they wanted to wear when they walked around the campus, and influenced how they came to work every morning and the fact that they wanted to try to build something great.

At certain moments that's what we have been able to do. You think of the stories we tell and the messages we deliver as being targeted at the audience that is ultimately going to purchase the product, but some of the coolest things we've done have been messages that inform the company and the people who work for the brand.

Pedigree is one of my favorite examples of that. Those people didn't understand the idea of being a company that loved dogs. They were a package-goods company that happened to be in the dog food business. We said "Why don't you be a company that loves dogs?" We served them up a manifesto that said "Everything we do is for the love of dogs." We came up with the shelter dogs program. It's made them the number-one dog food in the world, and when we're doing the shelter dog campaign, they sell more food than when we're running product commercials. We gave them a soul.

The stories we tell can ultimately affect a lot of different audiences. That's a pretty big part of what we do. Sometimes we even put a stake in the ground and say "OK we're going to say these things, you had better live up to them." And sometimes it helps companies to stretch and to do more. I always say that I think sometimes we have more ambition for our clients than our clients do.

The other edge of the sword is that the audience has the ability to call you on anything that offends them about who you are, what you say and what you sell. The thing we told Pepsi when we did "Refresh" was that this has to be totally transparent and the democracy of the internet has to guide it. This cannot be just a promotion from a soda pop company—you can't bullshit people and say you're doing one thing while you do something else.

ON PLANNING . . .

As an industry we also have to look at reinventing planning. We have got to reinvent the intellect of our business so that it is dedicated to the media world, to the connections in brand storytelling that are necessary in a world where everyone's an audience, everyone is a critic, and everyone has a voice. The total understanding of that cultural anthropology has to do with how people are living with media and how they're interacting with brands and how you have to tell your stories. If it's only coming from the creative guys it's framed as "Oh, the creative guys, they always want to do this."

We have got to reinvent the intellect of our business. The intellect of our business used to be planning—which Jay Chiat brought here from England—but it's now totally defunct. It doesn't do anything that needs to be done in this day and age. We have to be the experts in the room in how people hear messages, consume messages, think about brands and react to brands. That's the biggest thing that's missing right now because clients don't know what they're talking about. They know they want something else, they know there's some kind of new media landscape they're supposed to operate in, but they don't know what that means. They don't know what they're supposed to do.

And we're not being very helpful in telling them the mechanics of how their brand needs to operate out in the media world. The other thing that's totally broken is the old media company model. We find the idea that then dictates how a brand should behave out there in the paid and unpaid media world, and orchestrating that behavior is one of the most creative things we have to do, and if it's over at some other media company, that's a problem.

Historically, you give your budgets to the media company, and you take a percentage and give it to the agency to do the creative part. But as far as I'm concerned, we should also get 20 percent of the media budget because we're creating media! When we create content for the internet, we're creating media. And what they give us now is a production budget. They say "Film isn't in the production budget." This isn't a film, this is media, this is an idea that's going to get millions of hits for your brand. And you don't have to pay a percentage for the media, you just have to create content that will attract that kind of attention.

The impediment to some of this new creativity is the understanding of the client. We need to become better at educating them about thinking of media not in terms of the old model, but in terms of the new model. The new model, my model, is give me more money and we'll create some cool stuff that people will talk about. You don't have to put it on ABC or NBC.

Half these clients think this is somehow an economic move. They think it's a way of spending less money on marketing. Instead of understanding that it's a new model that, when understood and used well, can save money and have a bigger impact. Marketing isn't an expense; it's an investment in how the world sees a company.

ON TECHNOLOGY

When they invented the camera, in 1813 or whenever, it was technology. It was all amazing lenses and emulsions and "Whoa, I don't understand that." When technologists took cameras and did demonstrations, people thought it was magic.

It was technology and magic. The people that traveled around with cameras for the first 50 years were technologists. They weren't artists. You didn't see painters throwing away their canvases. For years photography was tech. It kept getting better, easier to use. Ultimately, someone said, "Instead of standing those people in front of that barn, you could put them over here. And if you wait until four or five in the afternoon when the light comes from over here, that could be a nicer image." So pretty soon photography was art. I think that's where we are with all this new tech. It's so controlled up to this point by technologists and digital guys. Clients are so mystified by it, because it's magic, so they go to the digital guys to tell them how to use it. But the

artists are just starting to figure out how to use it to tell stories to engage people and make them feel things as well as hear and see and
learn things.

I try to hire enough young people to solve these issues that I can
identify but am too old to resolve. It's neat that I still get to go and
work with a bunch of young people and do amazing stuff and reinvent who we are and how we do it. . . .

When I went to work with Jay Chiat, and he created these high
bars inasmuch as he wouldn't just let us imitate; we had to try to orig-
inate. What I loved was when I discovered that advertising was about
ideas and storytelling and not just graphic design for the sake of making something beautiful. It was the totality of making a message or
telling a story. After that I just became a student of storytelling,
whether it was filmmaking or music. My passionate belief is that
when we do what we do well, it's art. I try to defend that and do it to
the point where I can point to it and say, "Did that make you feel
something . . . ?"

I was self-taught by observation to a large extent. Whether it
was watching Bill Bernbach or George Lois or whoever. I always had
an admiration for my peers. A lot of the media tries to get you to
bash your peers, but I've been a constant admirer of anyone in our
business who's trying to do something interesting—a constant de-
fender of Wieden or Goodby or Hegarty or Droga. I'm an admirer
and student of and champion of anyone who's trying to break rules.
I say try to learn from someone who's doing something well and try
to do better.

AND NOW A FEW WORDS FROM JEFF GOODBY

The copywriter, co-chairman and creative director of Goodby Silverstein & Partners talks about what's changed, and what hasn't, in advertising, the digital rebirth of his agency and getting inside people's heads.

I think advertising has changed quite a bit. It's popular to say that "oh, it's still the same; we're just coming up with ideas." But it's changed.

What's the same is that doing an ad is always like setting a tone where people go, "Yes, she's like me, you know?"

I remember being in college and reading Volkswagen ads in magazines. They were really different from advertising that came before them because they were disarmingly like the way that you thought inside your head. They acknowledged that VW is an ugly little car built by Germans, who we didn't particularly like, because the war was only seven or eight years behind us at that point. Bernbach and Phyllis Robinson and Julian Koenig invented that sort of recognition, that sort of alarming intimacy. That's what I would call it, an alarming intimacy that makes you go, "Wow!"

That sort of alarming feeling that a person knows what you are thinking. It's a very powerful posture for a writer to be able to construct, if it's credible. And it's as true or false as human behavior is. It's true in advertising now and in internet experiences. You see things and you just go, "no, that's not the way I think about things," or you go, "Yes, they knew what I was thinking, or what I would find interesting."

A lot of advertising is understanding what that person might be thinking, and how far can I take that to another place? And how will I do that? And sometimes you find people trying to do things that are just impossibly far; you just can't make lightning snap between those two antennae. But every once in a while you find that you can do it, and make it move quite a ways.

It was probably hard for Helmut Krone [the art director who worked on VW at DDB in the 1960s] to make ads that were so pared back, so naked and appealing. And you know, the things that we do now are hard to come up with too, but they're complex. It's rare that you see simple experiences like that work anymore. Today we have to think about your media habits as well as your beliefs about a product. That alarming intimacy can happen, a lot of times, just because you got the medium right.

Lately my big soapbox has been that the things that our industry honors, and maybe the world honors, are new forms of things, in a Twitter and Facebook sense, and not really the craft.

We're kind of lucky [at Goodby Silverstein & Partners] because we had a little bit of the gene of new forms in us all along. When we first went into business we didn't have enough money to do beautiful commercials, even though the whole world was honoring that and doing hundreds of thousands of dollar kinds of productions. We started shooting things on the bad video cameras that existed, and then making them worse by projecting them on walls and reshooting them so that they'd look really grungy and ugly. And we thought that that was cool. In a way doing things like that was a craft, but it wasn't precious. It wasn't like "god this person looks great in this frame." And we made the music in our basements and stuff. And then the Chevy's Mexican Restaurants thing we did, where we made commercials and threw them away the same day, was probably the ultimate example of that.

That was an early example of the form being ahead of the craft— as opposed to today's technology, because you and I could make a commercial here and throw it away in an hour—it was a pretty crazy thing to do. And it was kind of a similar little frisson of excitement that we could do that, and just toss it out.

So my thing lately is that maybe what we're doing is moving into an age where—I'm not going to say that we don't love craft, because we still do—but maybe it's not the craft that drives us now. I think that the thing that really drives us is to come up with new forms. They don't need to be stunning in their craft, and it's more like you see something and go, "boy, where did that come from?"

It's kind of Darwinian, you know? Do you really need somebody to write 15 or 20 paragraphs of coherent copy? You don't. You really need another kind of person. So I think that the people who are lamenting the loss of that first kind of craft are lamenting something that is a very rare event in today's advertising, which is "I need this whole page of newspaper ad in the *Wall Street Journal*." I'm much more likely to need somebody to create a car web site that is about space, as in, I "want you to think about space as an abstraction, and what does it mean to people to have space and be able to move in space." And so the kind of brief we give out is much wackier than we used to give out.

I mean when I worked for Hal Riney—writing long things with subheads and cogent arguments and so on—I don't know how relevant that is today.

In a way I feel like the work isn't about a campaign now. We put out something that is like a novel without words. But the plot of it and the complexity of it are like a Balzac or something. You invent characters, they have lives, they think stuff, they do things. And sometimes it involves a lot of writing and sometimes it doesn't. But it's complicated. It started that year that we did the thing with the aliens coming down to Earth to take the cows away [an integrated campaign for the California Milk Processor Board that revolved around cow abductions]. And I thought to myself, this is like a novel. To put this out, like we're doing an alien web site, we're doing a farmer's web site for the farmers that are having their cows stolen, we're doing commercials about the drama, we're doing a three-minute piece that appeared in cinemas that had the whole story that all the commercials told, but told all in one story. We're doing posters that we put out on the landscape from cows that have been abducted. And people are looking at them and going "what the fuck is that?" It's a lot of moving parts. I'm sure everybody's saying this, but it's like writing a novel every week. It's like coming up with a whole little piece of drama.

IS TECHNOLOGY DRIVING THINGS . . . ?

I think smart people still have an idea what they want to achieve first. It's rather shallow to go "look there's an opportunity to do a Facebook page and get people to respond to it," but not have an idea of what that response should be or why you're getting that response. We need to have an idea what we want to accomplish first.

It makes sense to come up with a Nike+, but only when you know that what you want to do is involve people in running at a higher level. I think they had an idea what they wanted to accomplish before they came up with the experience.

There's that Museum of London thing that I liked this year, with the augmented reality app that allows you to hold your iPhone up and see what London used to look like hundreds of years ago in all these different locations. That's really engrossing, and a great technology, but you don't come up with it unless you know what end result you're trying to achieve. It's not just a trick, it's not just a small-minded kind of colorful gadget—it's something that actually works.

ON GOODBY'S DIGITAL TRANSFORMATION . . .

Part of the reason why Goodby Silverstein & Partners is an example of that is we were such a "traditional" agency to begin with. That means that we had a big picture window to throw a brick at. So when we did, I think the changes were really large. We also wanted it to happen fast. And it came down to hiring people who thought that way much more than any kind of ingenious environmental change we created.

It certainly changed a lot of the things that we were known for, such as meticulously planned TV spots and meticulously written print ads. And yes, we still lament the fact that we only have a few of these at the end of every year. But we're not obsessed with that anymore.

A lot of the new people we brought in were digital nerds, people that just loved the internet before other people loved it. And when they got into the milieu of our place, they blossomed. I think of people like Will McGinness, who is just a really talented guy but he was an internet nerd before anybody else was.

Those guys are incredibly valuable for creating an environment where that stuff is honored and celebrated. But at the same time, I think they have benefited by being in the middle of the craft, and being in an environment that's a little less ephemeral and a little more thoughtful.

I think the writers found it harder than the art directors. Which is weird, because writers should be storytellers. I mean, these are still stories; there's still a connection between what we did in the '60's and what we do now. And you would think that the writers would adapt to new media forms easily, but they didn't. They hold onto things pretty hard.

The visual people came along quicker. I think. Maybe if you're a visual person, you don't have quite so many preconceptions about beginning, middle and end, and experiences and stuff. I think. So in many ways, they were more useful for a bit.

And a different kind of writer has evolved, who, exasperatingly, can't write in the way that I was taught to write. They're not always grammatical and clear.

I still believe that some of the most interesting people we've hired over the years are people that don't come from advertising and have backgrounds outside of advertising. We were hiring people that are improvisational comics and stuff. But they're very different people. It's a much more open-minded world, I think, than it used to be.

ON STRATEGISTS . . .

I do think that in some ways, the complexity of technology, the things that we all have to deal with in media, have created a new kind of person that is sensitive to media, but also sensitive to the kind of beliefs that people have. And this person can put those two together. And that person didn't exist in advertising ten years ago, really.

In the old days it was like how does this guy hear about this message? You know, he watches it on TV; he hears it on the radio. But they didn't really analyze the possibilities of each of those media and figure out, what it can do and why it's different and how we digest it. But now people that think that way are succeeding. They think in terms of the medium as the message. And we have a big demand for them, but you can see that we don't necessarily have a big supply of them. They're coming, but they're not here yet.

And one of the things that I constantly do is implore them to interact with the creative people, because I think that most agency planners don't actually talk to creatives, or affect the creative works. They talk to clients, and the clients feel comfortable. But they're really afraid of the creative people. And one of the things that we have done for years is to have the planners talk to the creative people. I mean, that's even more important now.

I think a lot of times the function of a strategist nowadays is like kindling, you know? It's like intellectual kindling—making us really fascinated with this area that yesterday didn't seem very interesting.

I love things that involve. You know, like the Nike basketball challenge that they did. Where you could contact people over the internet and get pickup games of basketball at various playgrounds? I love stuff like that, that connects the real world with a product. It's truly useful stuff.

I like it when we have a purpose that is clean and pure and interesting and useful. You don't always have that. Often, you're trying to dramatize, like "refreshes every part of you," or something.

NOTES

I interviewed over 50 copywriters and professionals for this book. Their quotes are used throughout.

CHAPTER 1: THE CREATIVITY AGE

1. The history or politics buffs among you might associate the phrase "Best and Brightest" with the 1972 book *The Best and the Brightest* by David Halberstam, who used the titular expression ironically to describe the cadre of tragically arrogant members of JFK's inner circle, who, ignoring the advice of their more experienced predecessors made a series of terrible decisions that deepened the Vietnam quagmire. While we can presume that *Esquire* was using the term earnestly, anyone studying or working in the novelty-obsessed advertising industry will do well to bear the historical usage in mind.

2. "Old bastards" is not an inexcusable bit of ageism. Old bastards does not necessarily speak of chronological age, but rather attitude. It's a closed attitude that prefers things the way they were, that can't be bothered doing the work of evolving. There are lots of "old bastards" who are under 40 and lots of future-facing people well over that age.

3. A ridiculous, almost infinite number of books on "the industry" are published each year. Ignore nearly all of them. You've got too much else to read. Some of the titles you might actually want to pay attention to are listed here. Some of them are not necessarily about the industry. They are about social, cultural and technological changes that require attention.

   For a fantastic, all-round account of why creativity matters more than ever today: *A Whole New Mind: Why Right-Brainers Will Rule the Future,* by Daniel Pink (New York: Riverhead Books, 2005).

   For an exceedingly intelligent examination of the origin and meaning of social media and the impact of digital technology on the way people behave in general: *Here Comes Everybody: The Power of Organizing without Organizations,* by Clay Shirky (New York: Penguin, 2008) And for what that change in behavior means to society *Cognitive Surplus: Creativity and Generosity in a Connected Age,* by Clay Shirky (New York: Penguin, 2010).

For the most raunchy and brilliant novel that has anything what-ever to do with the ad industry: *Money,* by Martin Amis (New York: Penguin, 1986)

If you just need something great to read and haven't read it yet: *Blood Meridian: Or the Evening Redness in the West,* by Cormac Mc-Carthy (New York: Vintage, 1992).

4. If you want to take a liberal view, the origins of advertising, arguably, go back to cave paintings, or at least, as Mark Tungate notes in *Adland: A Global History of Advertising* (Philadelphia: Kogan Page, 2007), to Roman times. But the first real ad agencies formed in the mid-1800s.

5. Jeff Howe, "The Rise of Crowdsourcing: Why the Power of the Crowd Is Driving the Future of Business," *Wired,* June 2006, http://www.wired.com/wired/archive/14.06/crowds.html?pg=1&topic=crowds&topic_set=.

CHAPTER 2: BERNBACH TO THE FUTURE

1. David Ogilvy, *Ogilvy On Advertising* (New York: Vintage Books, 1985), 24.

2. Except in his spare time—Rosser Reeves was actually a poet and short-story writer in his off hours.

3. *The Art of Writing Advertising: Conversations with Masters of the Craft* (Chicago: NTC Business Books, 1965), 118.

4. Howard Gossage, *The Book of Gossage* (Chicago: The Copy Workshop, 1995), 19.

5. The early female ad pioneers were fewer in number but influential. They included:

Phyllis K. Robinson, one of the original copywriters at Doyle Dane Bernbach and author of some of the agency's most famous work for Levy's and Orbach's stores.

Shirley Polykoff, who, in 1956 practically invented the home hair-color industry, writing the lines, "Does she . . . or doesn't she? Only her hairdresser knows for sure," and "Is it true blondes have more fun?" She was the only female copywriter at Foote, Cone & Belding in 1955 when she was assigned the Clairol account.

Mary Wells Lawrence, another copywriter at DDB. In 1966, she founded Wells Rich Greene, an agency responsible for some of the most enduring ad slogans ever, and gained fame for her whole-brand approach to launching Braniff Airlines.

6. Daniel Pink, *A Whole New Mind: Moving from the Information Age to the Conceptual Age* (New York: Riverhead Books, 2005).

7. Michael Lewis, *The Big Short: Inside the Doomsday Machine* (New York: W. W. Norton, 2010), 11.

8. "*Dark Knight* final tally even bigger," *Variety,* July 20, 2008, http://www.variety.com/article/VR1117989210.html?categoryid=13&cs=1.

9. *The Art of Writing Advertising,* 23.

CHAPTER 3: THE STORYTELLERS

1. Scott Donaton, *Madison and Vine: Why the Entertainment and Advertising Industries Must Converge to Survive* (New York: McGraw-Hill, 2005), 101.
2. BMW demographic information from iMedia Connection. Tom Hespos, "BMW Films: The Ultimate Marketing Scheme," July 2001. http://www.imediaconnection.com/content/546.imc.
3. Ibid.
4. Sean Stewart's blog post on The Beast, http://www.seanstewart.org/beast/intro/.

CHAPTER 4: DIGITAL IS NOT A CHANNEL

1. From CPB's estimates, http://wwwawards.cpbgroup.com/awards/subservientchicken.html.
2. Read it here, it's recommended reading for anyone doing anything digital in the brand world, http://www.barbariangroup.com/posts/1938happy_5th_birthday_subservient_chicken.
3. Full-service agencies have different approaches to how much technical capability they have within their walls as full-time staff. Initially, agencies kept only an expanded version of the creative and production teams and outsourced the really heavy technical lifting—i.e., the tech capability to build a huge, complex site for a big marketer. Many digital agencies, of course, have this capability in house. Recently, more full-service agencies have started to bring a bigger piece of this in house.

CHAPTER 5: HOW TO NOT WRITE ADVERTISING

1. Seth Godin on permission marketing, William C. Taylor, "Permission Marketing," *Fast Company*, March 31, 1998, http://www.fastcompany.com/magazine/14/permission.html.
2. Nicholas Car, *The Shallows: What the Internet Is Doing to Our Brains* (New York: W. W. Norton, 2010).
3. Sam Anderson, "In Defense of Distraction: Twitter, Adderall, Lifehacking, Mindful Jogging, Power Browsing, Obama's BlackBerry, and the Benefits of Overstimulation," *New York Magazine*, May 17, 2009, http://nymag.com/news/features/56793/.
4. Clay Shirky, *Cognitive Surplus: Creativity and Generosity in a Connected Age* (New York: Penguin Press, 2010).
5. Dave Trott, "The Difference Between an Insight and an Idea," *Brand Republic*, June 29, 2010, http://community.brandrepublic.com/blogs/dtb/archive/2010/06/29/the-difference-between-an-insight-and-an-idea.aspx.

6. As articulated by Robert Capps, "The Good Enough Revolution: When Cheap and Simple Is Just Fine," *Wired*, August 24, 2009, http://www.wired.com/gadgets/miscellaneous/magazine/17–09/ff_goodenough.

CHAPTER 6: LIFE IN ADLAND

1. David Carr, "A Cultural Artifact, on the Block," *New York Times*, May 30, 2010, http://www.nytimes.com/2010/05/31/business/media/31carr.html?_r=1&partner=rssnyt&emc=rss.
2. "How This Ad Recession Compares," *Advertising Age*, December 3, 2009.
3. Kunur Patel, "Wrigley Drops Tribal DDB, Digitas and Agency.com for Digital." AdAge.com, November 10, 2009, http://adage.com/agencynews/article?article_id=140417.
4. The upfronts are an annual spring ritual wherein TV networks throw huge celebrity-studded events to preview their upcoming programming to media buyers, who negotiate what marketers will be paying for air time that season. Weird, huh?
5. Jeff Beer, "When Vice is Virtue," *Creativity Online*, March 2009, http://creativity-online.com/news/when-vice-is-virtue/135398.
6. Nick Parish, "Q&A with Jae Goodman," *Creativity Online*, July 14, 2006, http://creativity-online.com/news/qa-with-jae-goodman/123787.
7. Advertising has been one of many industries to embrace unorthodox job titles; you'll find real people in the business with titles like chief instigator, chief happiness officer, or ninja something or other (when Alex Bogusky moved from overseeing creative at CPB, his role at holding company MDC was chief insurgent).

   As painful as it is, perhaps the underlying phenomenon should be considered welcome; roles are blurring, companies are moving past the structures that governed advertising in the TV era.

   Notwithstanding ninjas and insurgents, the above described roles are still among the more significant others that will be involved in your day-to-day life. There are many others.
8. Jeremy Mullman, "Think Twice before Axing Account Management," *Advertising Age*, April 26, 2010, http://adage.com/agencynews/article?article_id=143494.
9. You can download Habberstad's well-regarded "Anatomy of Account Planning" on the site of the Royal Society of Account Planning, http://royalsocietyofaccountplanning.blogspot.com/2009/05/welcome-welcome-lets-start-with-anatomy.html. You can also find there a link to download "The Account Planning Group's Definition of Account Planning."
10. The five-tool player in baseball can hit for average, hit for power, run bases with skill and speed, field well and throw. Willie Mays was a five-tool player.

11.   Hillary Chura, "McDonald's Pulls Further Away from Mass Market-
      ing: CMO Larry Light Calls for Move to 'Brand Journalism,'" *Adver-
      tising Age,* June 16, 2004, http://adage.com/article?article_id=40403.
12.   Bruce Horovitz, "'Two Nobodies from Nowhere' Craft Winning Super
      Bowl Ad," *USA Today,* December 31, 2009, http://www.usatoday.com/
      money/advertising/admeter/2009admeter.htm.
13.   Jeff Howe, "The Rise of Crowdsourcing," *Wired,* June 2006, http://www
      .wired.com/wired/archive/14.06/crowds.html.

CHAPTER 7: BRINGING IDEAS TO LIFE

1.   Jeremy Mullman, "Dos Equis' 'Most Interesting Man' Is an Even
     Greater Beer Salesman," *Advertising Age,* July 15, 2009. http://adage
     .com/article?article_id=137963.
2.   Lieberman speaks of *George Washington,* the animated film by the as-
     toundingly talented writer Brad Neely, who also made videos saluting
     JFK and biblical history.
3.   Amazingly, the Ford F Series truck was the top-selling vehicle every
     year from 2000 to 2009.
4.   Abbott says, "When I first did that ad it was a baby; it said the car will
     fall on the baby. The client winced at that. The next season we showed
     the ad and we showed the welder under the car. They said we can't do
     that, the trade unions would go mad. The next season we showed it
     with me lying under the car. No one seemed to mind. You have to be
     tenacious."
5.   Would David Abbott get a job in copywriting today? http://www
     .campaignlive.co.uk/news/173211/DAVID-ABBOTT-JOB-ADVER-
     TISING-TODAY/.
6.   In the U.K., marketers and media buyers traditionally used the Na-
     tional Readership Survey's classification of magazines' readers. ABC1
     refers to the higher-ranking demographics according to job description
     and socio-economic status.

CHAPTER 8: IT'S JUST GETTING GOOD

1.   Natalie Zmuda, "Pass or Fail, Pepsi's Refresh Will Be Case for Market-
     ing Textbooks," *Ad Age,* February 8, 2010, http://adage.com/digital/
     article?article_id=141973.

INDEX